AF615271

SOFTWARE QUALITY ASSURANCE AND EVALUATION

SOFTWARE QUALITY ASSURANCE AND EVALUATION

JAMES H. DOBBINS

SOFTWARE QUALITY ASSURANCE AND EVALUATION

James H. Dobbins

Library of Congress Cataloging-in-Publication Data

Dobbins, James H.
Software quality assurance and evaluation / James H. Dobbins.
p. cm.
Includes bibliographical references.
ISBN 0-87389-059-0
1. Computer software—Quality control. I. Title.
QA76.76.Q35D63 1990
005—dc20

Acquisitions Editor: Jeanine L. Lau
Production Editor: Tammy Griffin
Cover design by Walzak Design. Set in Century Schoolbook by Carlisle Communications. Printed and bound by BookCrafters.

ISBN 0-87389-059-0

10987654321

Quality Press, American Society for Quality Control
310 West Wisconsin Avenue, Milwaukee, Wisconsin 53203

Printed in the United States of America

DEDICATION

To Dr. Michael Fagan for his many hours of discussion, inspiration and exchange of ideas; to Bob Buck for all the things we accomplished together, so many of which are incorporated into this text; to Tom McCabe for opening my eyes many years ago to the need for measurement and evaluation; to my lovely wife, Mary Beth, whose support is never wavering and whose advice I always find so valuable; and to Nathan, our son, who is just beginning his life in this world and who makes me wonder what he will one day think of the work we are now doing.

CONTENTS

COMMENTARY

A book of this nature needs to be read, understood, and the concepts applied by a much wider range of disciplines than just quality assurance.

If there is one thing wrong with this book, it is the title. Within the software arena two "camps" have surfaced, each claiming to have supremacy over the other: software engineering and software quality assurance. These camps often fail to recognize that both play coequal major roles in the development of quality software that meets or exceeds user expectations and requirements. Therein lies the problem. Software quality assurance personnel will read this book. Software engineering personnel will, by and large, perceive that this book because of its title is of little or no value to them.

Japan has established the national goal of obtaining 30 percent of the U.S. software market by the 1990s. They intend to do this by applying the same discipline to their software products as they already do to their hardware products. We have already seen the inroads into the U.S. economy that Japan can make. Are we willing to surrender another industry, the domestic software industry, to them?

The principal theme incorporated into the Department of Defense software standards (DoD-STD-2167 and DoD-STD-2168) and reflected in the software pamphlets produced by the Air Force Systems Command, is that software quality is obtained by planning and building in quality *and* by planning and performing quality evaluations. The associated tasks necessary to do this are defined independent of organizational structure, but do require the involvement of engineering, quality, and management disciplines. The documents also employ the concept of relationships between the process and the product to improve overall quality. The process used to develop software must be understood and manageable. The products must be evaluated to determine initial quality and identify which aspects of the process can be improved to improve software product quality.

Which brings us back to the subject of this book, *Software Quality Assurance and Evaluation.* This topic is inherently of interest to those professionals actively involved in assessing the quality of software products. The approaches, concepts, and tools described can be helpful in identifying "holes" in existing software quality programs, and providing additional methods that may be incorporated to improve the software quality program.

This topic should also be of interest to those professionals involved in software engineering and management. By gaining an understanding of what software quality activities can do, engineering and management can better appreciate quality assurance's role, and be able to better incorporate the quality discipline into their respective activities. By working together, quality assurance, engineering, and management can identify and implement those process changes that will keep the U.S. software industry in the dominant position in the world's marketplace.

The challenge exists. Do we relearn the lessons that we so ably taught and apply them now, or do we wait and apply them after we have lost the battle?

Anthony F. Shumskas
Lt. Col. USAF
Office of the Undersecretary of Defense
Research and Development
The Pentagon

Mr. Dobbins' book presents a practical and comprehensive methodology integrating management and technical techniques for the purpose of consistently producing high quality software. Mr. Dobbins takes readers step-by-step through the application of diverse technologies. He addresses the various software production phases, the events, and activities which take place during the software production process, and the controls and management practices which determine performance. This book is a valuable working tool for everyone involved in the production and/or procurement of software products. It is must reading—an excellent book.

Dave Siefert
Corporate Quality Assurance, CSP
Advanced Quality Systems, World Headquarters
NCR Corporation

Alvin Toffler wrote a book called *Future Shock* that described the paralyzing effects advances in technology can have on society. In the software quality assurance (SQA) world, the wise manager and engineer must keep abreast of the incredible advances being made in software development philosophy and technology with equal advances in the way he/she measures the quality of the software produced by such technologies.

This book is very helpful. The discussions provided deal with the very latest issues in computer-aided SQA, quality measurement, and SQA management. Mr. Dobbins draws on the expertise he has gained from more than 20 years in the field of verification and validation to show how a properly administered SQA activity can be shown to save literally millions of dollars in developmental costs.

Many companies have realized, through hard experience, that SQA is never an option. In these companies SQA usually is well-funded. For those readers who do not have the privilege of working for such enlightened management, the information provided in this book will prove more valuable than many expensive seminars. It provides methodologies and approaches based on systematic analysis of modern case studies that give a platform from which to sell proper SQA efforts.

Software may be partly an art, but it is surely competitive. SQA is becoming more automated and more professional in its staffing. Mr. Dobbins has created a winning manual for competing in this modern SQA environment.

Douglas B. Henderson
Manager, Software Configuration Management
Teledyne Corporation

Software quality assurance is an organizational activity whose mission is to move data processing from an individualistic approach to one encompassing software engineering principles. James H. Dobbins' book provides a road map for integrating software quality assurance into a data processing function. Mr. Dobbins' years of on-the-job software quality experience show in the practical tips and techniques included herein.

Software Quality Assurance and Evaluation puts emphasis on software procurement quality assurance activities. The quality relationship with contractors and subcontractors is described. The book also includes a chapter on U.S. government quality assurance standards. Any organization should find these contracting quality assurance guidelines helpful.

One of the strong points of this book is its discussion of the software inspection process. Mr. Dobbins illustrates how logic can be diagrammed to help in this analysis. The resulting information provides defect profiles to help organizations better understand the common characteristics of all software. Anyone interested in software quality assurance, particularly government contractors, should read this book.

William E. Perry, CQA
Executive Director
Quality Assurance Institute
Orlando, Florida

PREFACE

This book is intended to provide the fundamentals required for the establishment of a software quality assurance function, and to indicate the apparent direction of this discipline in the immediate future. It is acknowledged that the discipline of software quality assurance is changing rapidly, and that this text cannot therefore address more than the current state of the art for such an evolving field of endeavor, and attempt to foresee what immediate future directions might possibly be. It is, however, intended to be sufficient for providing a solid foundation in the subject, and for giving the practitioner a framework around which an active software quality assurance function can be established, and from which it can evolve.

There are some fundamental assumptions upon which this book is based. They are as follows:

- The software engineering department is concerned with the development of quality products, and is willing to incorporate effective methods and tools designed to increase the overall quality of the software development process, as well as the software product.

- There is both an expressed and an actual desire on the reader's part to achieve a truly effective software quality program.

- The software development team, or the software procuring activity, understands that high quality in software does not just happen by magic, but that it is the result of managing quality, and that management of quality cannot happen without visibility.

- Software quality assurance is a discipline which is an important part of the software development process. It is an active and integral part, and not an expendable ancillary activity.

- Software quality is not something which "someone else" does. It is everyone's job. A software quality assurance department, or function, does not have the total responsibility for product quality.

- The discipline of software quality assurance is evolving. Any software quality assurance function which is to become, or remain, effective, must also evolve. Stagnation in this discipline is the most effective guarantee of obsolescence.

With these factors in mind, it is necessary to first address the structure. The *assurance* of software quality in a large software development organization is usually the province of a department or function established for that purpose. For the purposes of focus, the term department will be used throughout this discussion, even though the task may be performed by a staff function, or by a functional set of departments, (depending primarily on the organization's size).

There are important relationships which the software quality assurance (SQA) department should have with the remainder of the development team. These relationships can be major factors in the department's effectiveness.

Two of the primary relationships are with software engineering and software development. Throughout this book, the terms software development department and software engineering department will be used. These are generic terms for, respectively, the department which will be responsible for development of the software (design and code), and the department which will be responsible for generation of the system and software functional requirements documents, and which also may be responsible for the systems level test after software development is complete.

CHAPTER 1

SOFTWARE QUALITY ASSURANCE ORGANIZATION

Independence

The software quality assurance (SQA) department, if it is to perform its function properly and effectively, should have a management reporting chain which is independent of the departments or functions which it will audit.

If the software quality assurance department is a part of the software development department, or if the software development department manager and the software quality assurance manager both report to the same person, there is a built-in danger of the fox watching the henhouse. The software quality assurance department must have the autonomy to provide independent assessment of the software development process, from a quality perspective, without being immediately controlled or constrained by those SQA is supposed to be auditing.

If the size of the organization precludes such independence, **special** care must be taken by the senior management team to assure functional autonomy in spite of organizational closeness. The commitment must be made and practiced at the management level. There have been, and still are, too many cases where the software quality assurance department is so tightly controlled by the software development or system engineering departments that the SQA department is sterilized. The SQA department becomes a facade which serves only to confuse or give a false sense of security to customers.

Actual Case Examples

Case 1: Company A, a large systems development organization, was a subcontractor to Company B, also a large systems development organization. Under the standards governing the contract, an SQA department in Company A was responsible for various quality assurance functions, including audits and documentation reviews for adherence to quality standards. In actual practice, the Company A system engineering department (to which the software development department also reported), with the concurrence of Company A's program manager, had such tight control over the SQA department that SQA personnel could not publish any finding, audit report, document review report or anything else without the system engineering manager's permission. Anything that system engineering did not want reported did not get reported. Thus, SQA never rejected a single product. It took a threat of contract cancellation, and some management changes, to turn this condition around.

Case 2: Company C, a large company, had an internal SQA department which had been so sterilized by the software development department, that the SQA manager had to request permission of the facility manager before SQA personnel could perform a quality review of contractual documents. He also had to ask and receive permission before he could cross the threshold of a software development manager's office—a permission often refused.

Case 3: In a situation similar to that in Case 1, two companies were teamed on a large development effort. Company A, the subcontractor, had the appearance of an SQA department, but SQA had little or no substance. The SQA department was unable to pass an initial audit, and did not even have so fundamental an item as a set of quality procedures. It took almost two years to turn the situation around. The SQA department, the program office and others, worked to get Company A's SQA department to a point where it was able to begin functioning as a real SQA department.

These are just a few of many examples, all real situations involving large companies which should have known better. All examples involve conditions where the stranglehold on the SQA department was so severe that SQA was reduced to a function in name only.

Structure

The structure of the SQA department, given that the SQA discipline should always be evolving, is double-layered, as a minimum. This means that the department operates on at least two levels: One level is the day-to-day level of performance in accordance with the published SQA procedures. The second level of operation is future-oriented. This level is planning for what lies ahead, trying to determine future directions in SQA for the next two to five years, and formulating the techniques, practices, and procedures which eventually will become part of the future standard procedures manual.

The majority of personnel should be operating at the first level. A relative few (perhaps only one or two) of the more senior people should be operating at level two. Those operating at level two will be responsible for a considerable level of communication, not only within the company, but also with others in industry who are actively engaged in the discipline of SQA. The exchange of ideas and practices with these other practitioners will serve to blend the ideas from within and outside of the company and help to steer the future of the SQA department in a way which is most reasonable for that particular company, department or organization.

This double-layered approach should not be used as a negative discriminating factor. There is nothing which should prevent some level of overlap, and nothing which should prevent a person operating at level two to periodically function at level one. In fact, this is important in order to prevent losing sight of the daily problems and situations, understanding how gradual evolution in the practice is being accomplished, and studying the impacts of changes in procedures and techniques within the SQA department and in the software development and software engineering departments.

Procedures

The SQA department should have a comprehensive set of written SQA procedures. This means more than thumbtacking a notice on a bulletin board (which has been done in some companies). The SQA procedures manual should be carefully planned, should address each level of activity to be performed by SQA, the processes to be employed and the resultant actions to be taken as a result of any given process.

This manual is important for at least three reasons. The internal SQA department day-to-day activity should be guided by some accepted set of procedures. New SQA department members should not be without such guidance. The software development and software engineering departments should have ready access to the manual and should understand exactly what is to be done by SQA and what is expected from their own departments. The implementation of the SQA procedures should never be a surprise to anyone. In addition, the software development and software engineering departments should review the manual. If there is any activity which should be added, or any point which is unclear, unacceptable because of a sound technical or business reason, or wrong, then that should be discussed with the SQA manager. Once this is accomplished, the manual should be signed by both software development and software engineering management as an expression of acceptance of the manual and of their responsibilities under those procedures.

The SQA manual should be comprehensive enough to be applicable across all projects. Individual project requirements may require some tailoring, or some additional special procedures, but the basic manual should be, in all but a few cases, the written expression of the SQA responsibility for a project. There should be a thoroughly consistent SQA approach for a given company or facility. In that way, in addition to the advantages for SQA itself, the programmers and engineers are always aware of their own and SQA's responsibilities related to quality—regardless of the project to which they are currently assigned.

Procedures Manual Content

Clearly, the SQA procedures' content will be, in some measure, dependent upon the company organizational structure, the software development processes, and the library control system employed. Appendix A is provided as an example of a table of contents for an SQA manual. It is therefore intended to be a basic guide (not necessarily comprehensive for all possible cases) for what should be the content of a rudimentary SQA manual of procedures.

As the SQA discipline evolves, as new government and industry standards are developed, and as automated tools are developed to assist these tasks, the manual's contents will have to be modified accordingly. Therefore, the SQA manual of procedures for every SQA department should be reviewed and updated at least annually.

There also should be, in appropriate instances, SQA trial procedures implemented. These trial procedures are the forerunners of later, more clearly defined and proven procedures which will become a standard part of the SQA manual. These trial procedures result from advances in SQA technology, development of automated tools, changes in software development practices, new government and industry standards, and other such events.

CHAPTER 2

INITIATION OF SQA ACTIVITY

SQA, if it is to be effective, must be implemented as early as possible in the software development process. This means the time of initial planning, or, in the case where there is a customer, at the time of the proposal's creation.

In spite of what many program managers believe, even if only privately, effective SQA practices can cut costs, and the sooner the SQA activity begins, the more cost-effective the SQA process will be. The key word is *effective.*

You cannot test in quality, and you cannot presume quality. It must be planned for, budgeted, and made part of the total software engineering process. It therefore makes no sense to exclude SQA from the proposal process. SQA should be an active part of every proposal team, and there should be a section describing effective software quality practices in every software development proposal submitted. The discussion in the proposal should address the software quality practices, procedures and tools, the evaluation and visibility which will be provided the customer, how the quality data will be collected and analyzed, how the quality data will be used as part of the management information system, and what the SQA practices and procedures are which will assure that all of these activities are performed properly. This should be addressed both for the prime contractor as well as any subcontractor relationships.

New Business Review Board

In most companies, there is a management team which reviews new business initiatives. This activity can be referred to generically as a new business review board (NBRB). It is usually made up of senior executives from the various disciplines, such as engineering, software development, finance, operations, marketing, etc. It has the task, among others, of determining what new business initiatives should be pursued. This may be the pursuit of some new internal initiative or a new contract. If a new contract, there must be a determination of the feasibility of success, and of the level of funds to be expended in the process of pursuing the contract.

These funds must be specially allocated, since other contracts cannot be charged for the activity of pursuing this new contract. Special monies must be allocated and all contract pursuit activity must be charged against these funds. It is important to understand that these allocations do not have to be confined to marketing. The SQA department should be provided with sufficient funds to participate in the initial review process, and to participate on the proposal team.

In order to determine when such activity is taking place, the SQA manager should be included as a recipient of the NBRB minutes, and should be a participant where appropriate.

Request for Proposal (RFP) Review

The RFP, also referred to as the solicitation, defines the task to be performed and requests a proposal from potential contractors. In the RFP, the quality requirements usually are stated, and the standards to be imposed on the contract are specified. The statement of work (SOW) task to be performed by the contractor, specified in the RFP, is supposed to be defined with sufficient clarity for a potential contractor to respond technically and financially.

SQA Review of RFP

SQA should review the RFP for an assessment of the quality requirements. They should determine if the quality requirements in the SOW (including the documentation and reporting requirements) are consistent with current internal quality practices, and if the deliverable items are those with which SQA is familiar. If there are any quality requirements which have been quantified in the RFP (e.g., a software reliability mean time between failure of 99.94) and especially if the method of computation is a requirement (such as the use of a specific statistical model or type of model), then there should be a determination of whether the technology exists internally to address this issue. If there are any concerns or problems, the proposal manager must be notified immediately. If what is requested is not technically sound, or if there is an apparent conflict in the requirements (e.g., two different government standards are imposed, but one has superseded the other), these issues have to be addressed with the agency requesting the proposal. The proposal manager normally will not be conversant enough with these issues to identify them, and the input from SQA will be important in ensuring these concerns are addressed at the proper levels. The addressing of the concern between the company and the agency issuing the RFP is done by the proposal manager, not SQA. SQA should never address the issues directly with the issuing agency unless specifically directed in writing to do so by the proposal manager.

Review Against Internal Procedures and Standards

SQA should review the RFP against the internal SQA procedures manual and against the internal company, division or facility quality standards and development practices (whichever is the appropriate level). These reviews will assist the proposal manager in determining if there are any unique conditions which might affect the internal standards for productivity, cause a change in internal procedures, or involve some other perturbation which has to be addressed before or during the proposal writing process.

Proposal Input

SQA should be a part of the proposal writing team and should provide input to address the quality issues as specified in the RFP. In far too many instances, SQA department personnel have never seen an RFP. While there has been a natural tendency on the program managers' part to delay the active participation of SQA as long as possible, often for reasons of cost, this tendency should be suppressed and eliminated. The earlier SQA becomes involved, the more SQA can contribute to the success and cost-effectiveness of the program. At this early proposal stage, potential problems, which might be excessively costly to address later, can be resolved at the beginning, never to arise again.

The program manager should expect SQA to provide proposal input that is concise, clearly written, technically competent, and which addresses the specific issues in the RFP.

The technical proposal should convince the procuring agency that the contractor is able, as a minimum, to do the job. The SQA input to the proposal should address each quality factor of the proposal. Failure to address a material item in the RFP can result in the proposal being rejected as non-responsive. If a specific standard is invoked, then SQA should address the company's capability to meet the needs of that standard, and refer to any applicable past experience in implementing that standard. If specific quality attribute requirements are imposed, then SQA should address the understanding of that attribute and how and why the company will be able to successfully meet the requirement. For example, if a specific software availability requirement is imposed, do not address this by explaining how reliable the system will be. Address *availability* if that is required, and *reliability* if that is required. SQA will have to show that there is an understanding of the issues, and that the issues can be addressed and the requirement met. If you cannot do so with the people and technology available, the SQA manager should immediately notify upper management. An alternative may be required, additional personnel brought in, or the program manager may need to submit a no-bid. As distasteful as a no-bid may be, it is better than having to tell the procuring agency six months later that you lied on the proposal and that you really cannot do the job, or a part of the job.

The technical proposal will be graded, and this technical grade will be compared to the score of other responders. Then the cost proposals will be reviewed and compared to the technical score. Once the SQA technical task is identified and formulated, it will be necessary to provide an estimated SQA budget for inclusion in the cost proposal. This is an important part of the process because if the budget is substantially below that required, there will be cost overruns for the SQA function, and if the task is overbudgeted, it may be a contributing factor in the company not being awarded the contract.

In determining the cost, the SQA budget estimate should be based on a task-oriented process. The SQA budget should not be a level-of-effort input unless there is no other choice. The more definitively the tasks can be specified, and cost estimated, the fewer surprises there will be at contract award time.

Although the old rumor of "it went to the lowest bidder" is sometimes true, the usual case in software or total systems development efforts is that there is a weighting factor built in and proposals are judged on both cost and technical competence. A very high technical score can tend to offset a slightly higher cost proposal. The better the job done in writing the technical proposal, including the part contributed by SQA, the higher the technical score will be. No section of the proposal is ever to be considered as irrelevant to the technical score. Appendix B shows an example of this sort of scoring which has been used by a non-DoD U.S. federal government agency when scoring contractor proposals.

CHAPTER 3
SQA PLANNING

Contract Quality Requirements Review

SQA planning begins, once the contract is let or the development task begins, with a contract quality requirements review. This is similar to the RFP quality requirements review, but is a review of the result of what has finally been resolved or negotiated, and is the basis for planning the SQA activity for the remainder of the contract effort.

The contract quality requirements review will result in a summary of the specific requirements imposed by contract, and therefore those which are legally binding on the contractor. These requirements must be met and the contractor will be audited for compliance with them.

Commercial Practice

In many instances, a commercial company will not be responding to an RFP, but will be anticipating a future market need. In such a case, there may be no customer input, and the development will be predicated on the marketing department deciding what to develop. The marketers will likely determine what they believe to be a future customer need, and produce what can more correctly be described as a "statement of probable user need" than an actual requirement.

If the situation is such that the development of this document is done and then passed to software engineering to develop, with no more involvement or responsibility on the part of marketing, there is created a situation which is ripe for wide-spread dissatisfaction. The marketers complain because software engineering does not deliver what they requested, and software engineering complains about ridiculous requests from marketing. Both complain to top management that the other is responsible for their own non-performance. Top management sees one thing: product is not being built and, therefore, revenue is not coming in.

The real truth is that both are doing the wrong thing, and software quality should be providing the environment to alleviate this situation. Probably no one is going to ask software quality to do this, and nearly everyone thinks it is none of software quality's business.

The solution lies in the concept of ownership. The marketing department produces a document, and then feels that it transfers ownership of that document as soon as they pass it to software engineering. Software engineering feels that once marketing has passed the document to them, they own it, and are expected to deliver whatever is included. Both are wrong.

What really needs to happen is to have a quality review of the marketing document itself, not by the quality organization alone, but by the software engineers and the marketing personnel together. The Inspection Process, described in Chapter 4, is an excellent vehicle. Using this technique, there should be a formal inspection of the marketing document by a team of marketers and software engineers. The marketing document should not be accepted by software engineering until it has successfully passed inspection. Ownership remains with marketing until this successful inspection milestone event is reached. Once reached, ownership is passed to software engineering, which has responsibility to deliver.

The bottom line is that however it is accomplished, marketing does not impose requirements without feedback from those responsible for implementing those requirements. The ones who should assure that this happens are those in software quality. They really do have an interest and a role to play in this process. They are responsible for assuring and evaluating the software quality engineering process, not just products, from requirements through final product delivery.

Internal Requirements

The internal quality requirements review should already have been done, and its results recorded. This should have formed a portion of the work which entered into the proposal input. The quality planning should be consistent with the overall planning done at the project level.

There are some automated project planning tools available which can make the entire planning task easier. One such tool is Master Planner[1] from Strategic Financial Planning Systems in Alexandria, Virginia.

Master Planner is the first natural expert system for the PC to provide project managers, planners, and analysts with the capability to plan and control complex projects easily and efficiently. The key value of Master Planner is its ability to automatically create a baseline plan based on a single computer screen display of descriptions of the type of work to be done.

Master Planner can look forward in time and evaluate the project schedule and cash flow constraints with sufficient accuracy and lead time to allow the project manager to develop viable alternatives while the most attractive courses of action are still open.

Maintaining cost and schedule control of major projects requires planning and budgeting tools which:

- capture progress as it happens;
- alert management to potential problems before they arise;
- provide expert solutions to those problems early enough for managers to take effective corrective action;
- accurately account for the complexities and uncertainties associated with the project development plan;
- use resource-based cost estimating techniques which can take advantage of the judgment of experienced planners, analysts, and managers;
- use parametric cost and schedule estimating techniques as an independent check of resource-based estimates;
- support both centralized and decentralized planning, control, and updates; and
- are easy to use and maintain.

Master Planner does all of these tasks in a matter of minutes in an easy and understandable manner.

Master Planner is designed to be used in the initial stages of a project to:

- develop and validate (within hours) the baseline plan, schedule and budget;
- develop estimates of schedule and cost risk associated with the baseline plan and budget; and

- publish detailed work plans, schedules, resource requirements and budgets at the beginning of the project instead of months after the project has started.

Once a project has started, Master Planner is used to:

- record progress updates to determine schedule and budget adherence;
- re-evaluate uncertainty and risk assessments;
- develop work around plans; and
- rebudget both the timing and amounts of money required to complete the project.

Master Planner consists of four major subsystems. They are:

1. Master activity library (MAL) subsystem. It is composed of:

    - Master activity library (MAL)—A data base which delineates the following for each activity:

        — tasks (what has to be done)

        — responsibilities (by whom)

        — directives (how and why)

        — data descriptions (technical data reporting formats)

        — staffing (who has review and approval responsibility)

        — schedule (when each task must be done and its relationships to other tasks)

        — cost (how much the task should cost, how much it is costing and the projected costs to complete)

        — characteristics of the activity which influence cost and schedule

- Editors to enter and update each MAL activity and its associated files (activity, logic, staffing, funding, tailoring characterizations, etc.).

- Logic software to verify the dependencies between activities in the master activity library.

2. Tailoring subsystem. This subsystem consists of expert system software to create a specific project tailored plan from the master activity library (MAL) for use by the user PC subsystem. The user describes the general characteristics of the proposed effort to the tailoring subsystem which then automatically selects activities from the MAL to build a network of activities for a specific project.

3. User PC subsystem. This subsystem consists of:

   - The project specific data base which contains all of the activities related to a specific project and their respective schedules, logic, staffing, costs, and references.

   - Editors to enter new project specific activities and update files. The editors allow the user to continually monitor and, if necessary, modify the schedule and cost for the project. By using the *diary* the user may interface directly with any one or any group of activities and monitor, change or append information about those activities. In addition, the user may keep track of telephone calls, correspondence and the like. These editors allow almost immediate interplay between the on-screen project network drawing and a multitude of other computer screens of information about the network and its individual activities.

   - Schedule analysis software to verify the sequencing logic of the plan and compute activity dates and schedules.

   - Report generation software which automatically, in a matter of seconds or minutes, compiles and produces various project reports, either directly on the computer screen or as printed output. Some examples are:

     — complete network drawings or subnetwork drawings

     — report listings for all or selected information

— Gantt charts for activities or time-frames (see Chart 3.1)

— milestone charts for selected activities

4. Network integration and distribution subsystem. This subsystem consists of the following:

- Disaggregation software to create office specific activity subnetworks (OSAS) for distribution to individual responsible agencies and offices.
- Integration software to compute the interactions between multiple projects.
- Network communications projects to distribute subnetworks of activities and upload project specific networks to a central mainframe or another PC.
- Report generation software to provide composite status reports and interaction reports for multiple users on the same project and for multiple projects which provide equipment to one another.

Within this overall planning capability will reside the SQA planning analysis, and the interrelationship of the SQA planning to the rest of the project plans and activities.

Budgeting

Part of the initial SQA planning is budgeting. The SQA task must be budgeted carefully. In the past, many SQA organizations have only paid lip service to the budgeting task. They relied on the software development, system engineering, configuration management, software test, and other departments to do all their budgeting first. Then SQA would submit their budget as a percentage of all or part of those other efforts. This is no longer an acceptable method of SQA budgeting. The SQA budget should be task-oriented, with each task separately accounted for and the cost computed separately.

The obvious dangers of the percentage method are that the initial start-up required for any contract, regardless of size, is never really considered, and the chance of the program manager making across-the-board cuts of budgets, including the SQA

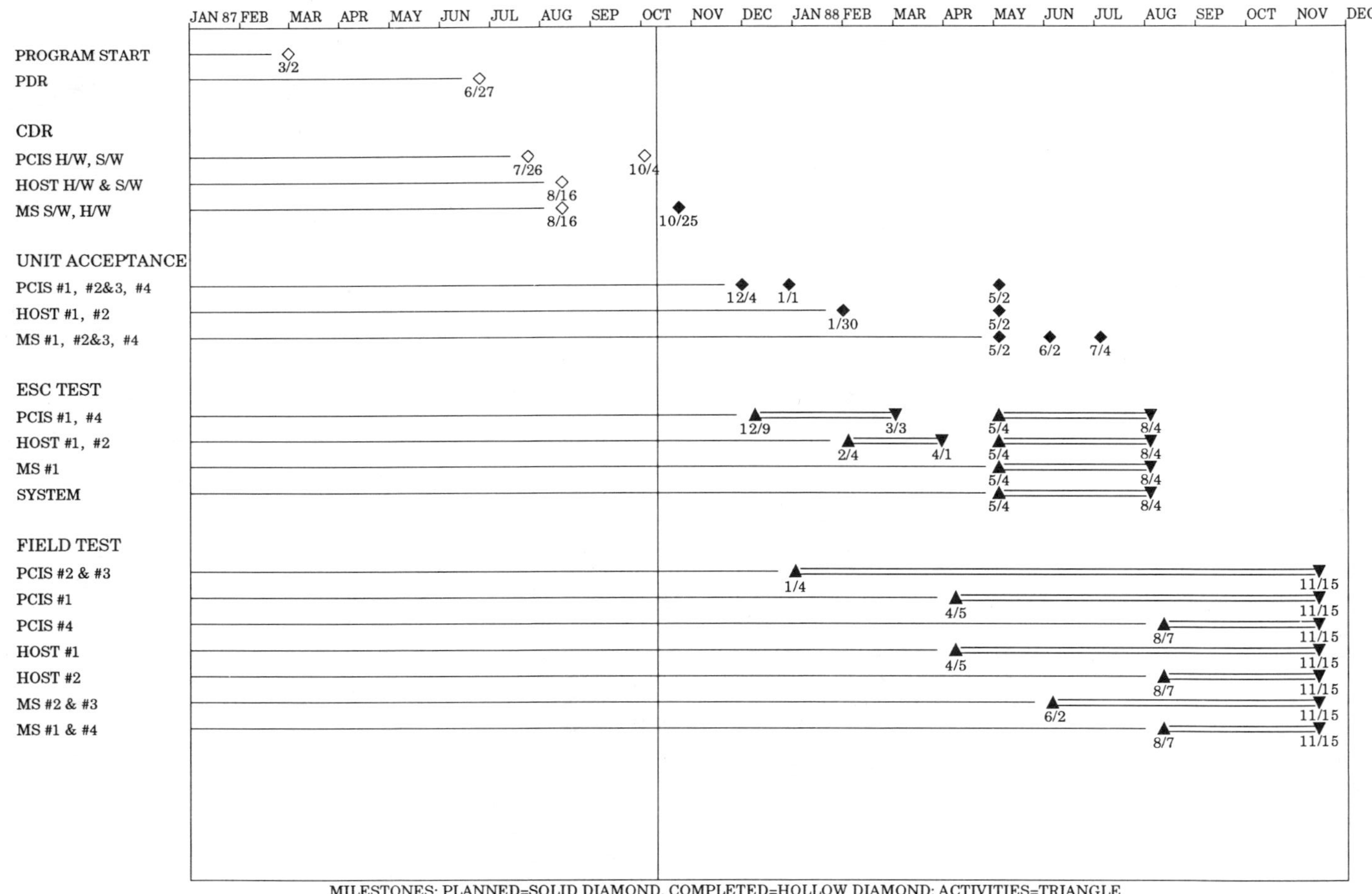

Chart 3.1 Master Planner Sample Milestone Chart

budget, is quite real. If the budget is percentile-based, an across-the-board cut will leave you with no argument. If the budget is task-oriented, the decision is left to choose which tasks or portions of tasks will not be done.

Most, or all, SQA tasks are mandated by contractual requirements. Some may be mandated by internal requirements. Some internal requirements have become contractual requirements because the internal standards were included as a reference in the contractor's proposal. Under such a condition, you may have a valid argument against a budget cut since the cut will mean that the company does not meet contract compliance, and the SQA function is one which invariably is audited by the customer (especially on government contracts).

You cannot propose to do a job, secure a contract on the basis of that proposal, and then refuse to provide the tasks proposed. If the customer is charged for services not provided, the condition is ripe for a charge of fraud against the company.

If a budget cut is necessary, the task-oriented budget serves as a basis for the program manager to further negotiate with the customer in an attempt to retain the full SQA level of activity. If it has to be cut, some contract requirements relief may be required. Without a task-oriented budget, none of this negotiation is possible.

SQA Cost Tracking

SQA cost tracking is the result of the work authorization and budget process working together. When the task is authorized the budget allocated for that task is then provided. This is based on the budget submitted for that task.

The SQA budget usually is tracked by both hours and dollars, because the budget may have been submitted, often in terms of hours, under the assumption that the work would be performed by a person charging according to a certain labor category.

If the actual work when the contract begins, or at some time thereafter, is being done by a person of higher or lower labor category level than that assumed by the budget, then the dollar expenditure will not be consistent with the budget hours according to the originally submitted budget.

If the new person is at a higher level, the hours may be consistent with what was budgeted, but the dollars may be in an overrun condition. Likewise, the opposite may be true.

This means that throughout the performance period, the SQA manager must track both hours and dollars for each authorized task. If either is not within a fixed percentage of the estimated expenditure for that given point in time, a variance notice requesting a variance report should be submitted to the department having the variance.

A variance notice is a monthly budget status report from the program office indicating that a variation in expenditure rate has been detected which exceeds the allowed percent deviation (typically 5 percent). It is sent to each work package manager responsible for a work task which is in a deviant condition. This notice should request a report analyzing the variance.

In this variance report, the manager is expected to explain why the variance exists and what will be done to correct the variant condition. A task-oriented budget makes this job much easier for the SQA manager than a percentage type budget. That is because the task budget makes it easier for the SQA manager to track the work efforts of individual department members as the contract proceeds through the various life cycle phases, since each major task will have its own work package number.

An estimate of the total expenditure in hours and dollars at completion of the work task is also expected to be included in the variance report. In this way, the program office will not only have a reason for the variance, but also will have an analysis of whether the condition will be brought within tolerance limits by the end of the task authorization period. If the variance report is properly completed, the program manager will have the visibility required to address significant issues as soon as they surface. If an underrun condition will persist, then the excess funds can be drawn back to the program office management reserve fund and utilized for areas experiencing the opposite situation. If an overrun condition exists, the situation can be dealt with (sometimes with customer involvement) as soon as it surfaces.

If the proper system is set up for tracking the time expended on individual tasks, as compared to the budgeted time, and compared to the type and size of the technical effort, the budgeting process itself can be continually refined. Thus, the budget task is made easier and more accurate.

SQA Budget Justification

On many contracts, especially government contracts, the contractor must submit a justification sheet for budgets submitted. This is to assure the customer that the figures presented as the required budget are not unfounded and to further serve as a negotiation basis.

A justification which is based on a percentile budget process is extremely difficult to justify, as it is classified as "level of effort." It is the easiest kind of budget to cut and negotiate down. The standard argument of "work smarter and harder," is hard to defeat.

On the other hand, a task-oriented budget is much easier to justify, especially if any sort of track record is established, and in negotiation the effort is centered on the tasks themselves. If the SQA budget is suggested for reduction, it becomes a question of which task(s) to eliminate. The customer is reluctant to eliminate any task designed to assure quality, as well he should be, especially when that task has been required in the RFP or negotiated budget.

The justification sheet, or "J" sheet is used for providing the SQA justification for the submitted budget, and can also be used as input for generation of the submitted budget data itself.

Appendix C is an example of what a J sheet might look like, and the resultant budget sheet which is computed based on the J sheet data. This was done using a standard spreadsheet program and is formula-driven. If the user inputs the data into the J sheet, defining what is to be done, the budget hours are computed automatically. When the justification data is computed, the resultant budget sheet (also formula-driven and referenced back to the J sheet file) is computed, giving a breakdown by task (by labor code), and showing the average hours per month (by labor code) for this effort.

Naturally, the budgeted tasks are driven by the required activity as well as the software development processes utilized at a particular location. They also are driven by the degree to which automated tools are employed. Therefore, the budget example shown in Appendix C should not necessarily be adopted as *the* budget process for the reader's location. It is provided to serve as a guide for what can be done to produce justification and budget sheets as easily as possible. It is important to note that since the SQA budget has to be justified, the scheme employed here is to create the task-oriented justification data first, and derive the budget from that. The program which has been developed to produce these budget sheets automatically creates the budget sheets from the justification data. Therefore, the budget always is justified since it is computed directly from the justification information.

Applicability Matrix

Part of the SQA planning process is to determine the extent to which the contractual requirements are met by internal standards and practices, and by the provisions of the SQA procedures manual.

One helpful method for determining this is to review all of the contractual standards, note the provisions of each, and cross-reference these provisions to internal standards and practices and the SQA procedures. This is best written in the form of a matrix, with the provisions of the contractual standards noted, by paragraph number, down the left side. The implementing counterpart from internal standards and SQA procedures should be noted in columns having the title of the applicable document at the top of each column. One column should be left open for the SQA plan, usually a deliverable item on government contracts.

Whether or not the software development effort is for a government contract, or purely for internal reasons, the applicability matrix is a good planning tool. For purely internal development, the internal company standards which are applicable to this type of development effort are treated as the contractual standards, and the SQA procedures are cross-referenced. Whether it is a deliverable document or not, an SQA plan should be written, and the provisions included in the applicability matrix.

For each item where the implementation requires, either by contract or internal standards, an activity which is outside the scope of the SQA procedures, a special program unique procedure may have to be written and either included in the SQA plan or in the SQA procedures manual as a special procedure. If the task is being performed under a contractual basis, the necessity for these special procedures should have been noted while in the process of the proposal's preparation.

By going through this cross-referencing as a part of SQA planning, the SQA department is assured of an accounting for all quality requirements of the contract or internal effort. If any quality requirements require special preparation, additional manning, or any other special condition, this will be known at the outset and can be included as part of the effort's overall planning.

Appendix D presents an example of how an applicability matrix might be structured.

SQA Evaluation Planning

Software quality evaluation is becoming an integral part of the current practice of SQA. It is increasingly important for several reasons, including:

- DoD-STD-2167A and DoD-STD-2168 require software quality evaluation.
- Businesses are being asked more often to warrant their software.

- The effectiveness of proposed new software development practices has to be evaluated.

- Visibility is required for total program management.

It is becoming increasingly important to evaluate software because of the management visibility required into the software development process at each life cycle phase. The development managers and, in today's environment, the procuring customers paying the cost of development, cannot wait until test phases begin if they are to get an understanding of the quality of the products under development.

The most cost-effective way to manage software quality is to determine the effectiveness of defect prevention and removal activity at every life cycle phase—from requirements generation through operation. This requires that there be measurable insight into the software development and change activity.

The measurements must be:

- meaningful;

- as pragmatic as possible;

- as simple as possible to implement;

- automated where possible;

- developed to evaluate both processes and product;

- implementable as early as possible in the life cycle;

- designed to cover every life cycle phase; and

- as nonintrusive on the programmers as possible.

Both the processes and products of software engineering, including specified aspects of software quality, must be measured. The process by which software is developed, or requirements are written, can have as large an effect on the final product quality as anything else. Therefore, both process and product measures must be implemented. The *visibility* afforded by the measures will provide the data and information required to *control* the development process. The control derived from proper visibility is the key to successful software development management. Both technical and cost management can be best achieved through the attainment of control afforded by meaningful visibility. This can be accomplished only through an effective and consistent software evaluation program.

Software Quality Factors

For each of the projects undertaken, whether under contract or otherwise, there will be certain quality factors which are important to that particular effort. For a nuclear reactor project, where safety is of paramount concern, the quality factors of reliability, integrity, and usability might be of primary importance. In the FAA project, the factor of availability is considered paramount. And so on.

The draft versions of DoD-STD-2168 identified quality factors as correctness, efficiency, flexibility, integrity, interoperability, maintainability, portability, reliability, re-usability, testability and usability. Definitions were provided for each factor. These factors were based on a paper written by Jim McCall,[2] one of the first people to describe quality in terms of a set of definable factors. It was at this time, for instance, that reliability was recognized as a factor of quality. Quality was seen as the umbrella which encompassed several factors which had often been thought of, and treated, as being quite separate from quality. The final published version does not specifically include these factors, but they are referenced in Appendix D of DoD-STD-2167A, and the Software Requirements Specification DID.

Quality Factors Determination

In attempting to determine which of the various quality factors should be incorporated on a given contract, there are several considerations. These considerations revolve around initial quality concerns and resultant application of the factors based on identified concerns and environmental characteristics. These can be shown in Charts 3.2 and 3.3. These charts are examples of the kinds of reasoning which must be done to determine the applicable quality factors, and therefore the kinds of reasoning which must be undertaken when proposing a tailoring of standards DoD-STD-2167A and DoD-STD-2168.

Acquisition Concern	User Concern	Quality Factor
Performance—How well does it work?	How well does it utilize a resource? What confidence can be placed in what it does? How easy is it to use?	Efficiency Integrity Reliability Usability
Design—How valid is the design?	How well does it conform to the requirements? How easy is it to correct/change? How easy is it to verify its performance?	Correctness Maintainability Testability
Adaptation—How adaptable is it?	How easy is it to modify? How easy is it to interface with another system? How easy is it to transport? How easy is it to convert for use in another application?	Flexibility Portability Re-usability Interoperability

Chart 3.2 Quality Concerns

Becoming accustomed to such a tailoring process will not be easy, but is necessary. Remember, these charts are examples, not a firm determination for all projects. They show the quality factors as they relate to specific concerns, and as they relate to user environmental characteristics.

By taking into account the kinds of considerations as expressed in these two charts, the user and the developer are able to arrive at the identification of those quality factors which should be identified for evaluation on the particular project. In this way, those quality factors which are important to the project are identified, and can be incorporated into the software quality evaluation plan (SQEP) for that program.

The user should make every attempt to identify the pertinent quality factors prior to the issuance of the RFP. If this is not done, and if DoD-STD-2167A and DoD-STD-2168 are invoked without tailoring, then the companies submitting proposals either will have to assume that all 11 quality factors are to be evaluated, and budget accordingly, or call for a bidders' conference where these issues can be clarified. Both of these last options are unnecessarily time-consuming and costly and can be avoided by the user simply taking the time initially to select the pertinent quality factors and identify them in the RFP.

Application/Environment Characteristics	Software Quality Factors
Human lives affected	Integrity Reliability Correctness Testability
Long life cycle	Maintainability Portability Flexibility
Experimental system or high rate of change	Flexibility
Experimental technology in hardware design	Portability
Many changes over life cycle	Flexibility Re-usability
Real time application	Efficiency Reliability Correctness
On-board computer application	Efficiency Reliability Correctness
Processing of classified info	Integrity
Interrelated systems	Interoperability
High system cost	Reliability Flexibility

Chart 3.3 Examples of Application/Environment Characteristics and Related Software Quality Factors

Software Evaluation Resource Planning

In planning the software quality evaluation process, the resources which will be allocated for the evaluation process must be identified. These include personnel, budget, and the tools and practices necessary to implement the evaluations. The organizational responsibilities for performing the evaluations also must be identified and commitments must be given to both performing the evaluations and utilizing the results. The software quality evaluations may not necessarily all be done by SQA, but SQA is the likely candidate for assuring that the evaluations are performed. As such, the commitment from those who are identified as responsible for performing the evaluations is critical to the success of SQA in meeting its responsibilities.

Quality Evaluation Criteria and Plan

Once the quality factors have been identified, the means to implement the evaluations must be determined. This means that the criteria for making the evaluation judgment must be decided upon, and then the means for assessing these criteria will be identified.

Once the quality evaluation implementation means have been identified, the criteria have been established, and the resources identified (including the tools and procedures required), the plan for implementation can be developed. This will include the identification of the quality factors, the life cycle phases during which the quality factors will be evaluated, how often the evaluations will be made, how the results will be interpreted, and to whom the data will be provided. It also will be necessary to periodically review the quality evaluation plan to determine if the factors, evaluation means, frequency, and life cycle phases for evaluation should be modified.

It is not unusual for the progress of a project to have an impact on the evaluation program, and therefore periodic review of the software quality evaluation plan is necessary. Initial planning, no matter how well done, should never be assumed to have been so perfect as to never require re-examination. The quality factors may change, the types and frequency of measurement may change, or the kinds of evaluation reports may have to be modified. The visibility required for intelligent insight into what the current situation may be, compared to the desired condition, will to some extent determine the changes which might be required. Either developmental difficulties or unexpected progress may have an impact on the changes to the evaluation program.

The quality evaluation criteria should be given considerable thought when establishing the evaluation plan. Any criterion against which a quality factor is evaluated should be one which is meaningful to the management team. Since an evaluation plan is intended to be used as a management tool, the results must be usable by management.

Criteria for evaluation should clearly identify whether the factor evaluated is what it should be, and indicate what action might be required if it is not what it should be. For example, if a given quality factor is evaluated at several life cycle stages, and if one of the evaluation measures for that factor is the module path coverage of the software test, then a criterion of effectiveness of the test might be test coverage of a certain percent. If the test evaluation criteria require a test coverage of 100 percent, and the test coverage evaluation indicates only 80 percent coverage, then the manager can understand what this means and take action to obtain test coverage of the remaining 20 percent of the software.

Software Quality Data Collection and Reporting

Part of the SQA planning process is a determination of the data collection requirements, and the evaluation analysis reporting requirements.

Data collection is determined by the provisions of the software quality evaluation plan (SQEP). The evaluation plan will specify the quality factors to be evaluated, the measurements to be taken, the evaluations to be made and by whom, and the reporting cycle. The SQEP will include all of the features of the quality data reporting system, including the results of audit reports, document reviews, configuration control elements, software procurement quality elements, and the like.

SQA should be the focal point of responsibility for quality data analysis and reporting. Since SQA is the likely point for determining and assuring that the quality evaluations are accomplished, the data resulting from the evaluations should be a part of the SQA data base. Quality data reports produced by SQA should be a composite of the evaluation results and the results of strictly SQA activity.

Since the reason for measurement is to obtain useful information for management control and product evaluation, the SQA data analysis and reporting should be as frequent as required for maximum utility. Implementation of the quality evaluation program is intended to afford the management team with the real time visibility and control required for effective technical and financial management. Data input from SQA must be timely enough to support this objective.

The SQA data reports must be such as to provide the management team, or the customer, with the information needed to perform their tasks effectively, but to also protect the identities of individual programmers.

The SQA data reporting should never become a club by which the management team evaluates individual programmers. The utility of at least some of the data is, to an extent, dependent on the willingness of the programmers and engineers to be measured. This means a certain level of exposure for them, and that willingness must be protected. The argument that a manager should be able to use the measurement data as an evaluation tool does not have merit. The manager should know his or her employees well enough to evaluate them without having to rely on details contained in the SQA data base. After all, managers have been doing just that for many years.

The SQA data reports should therefore be provided in summary form. Rather than report, for example, the defect densities of each individual software module, SQA can report on the composite defect density of all the modules evaluated during a particular period, to date for a specific time, or for a given facility, project or department. If a particular situation arises where the individual data is required, that should be handled at the management level as a special exception.

One of the requirements for the SQA reporting system is trend analysis. It is specifically required on government contracts, and is a requirement of government software specifications and standards such as paragraph 5.8.1.9 of DoD-STD-2167 and paragraph 4.1.9.d of DoD-STD-2167A.

A composite data reporting system is best suited to trend analysis, and the SQA data reporting system should be oriented in this way. One essential element of the reporting mechanism is that the data should be as current and complete as possible. Therefore, the software quality evaluation plan should incorporate provisions for providing the results of the evaluations to SQA immediately after the evaluation is performed.

SQA should always follow up with top management after publication of the report. It is often not feasible to do so on a one-to-one basis. It would be too time-consuming for both parties. However, the SQA reporting mechanism should include a presentation on the results of the analysis report at the regular program review meetings for each project. The SQA representative assigned to that project should make the report. The purpose is to assure the program manager that SQA is providing the services required, to answer any questions about the report, and to assure the management team that SQA is a contributing part of the development team. This requires that the person making the presentation be intimately familiar with the report contents and meaning. This also avoids the trap which occurs so often when one person in the SQA department performs all or most of the data analysis. That one person becomes the repository of the knowledge of the SQA data for the different projects, and the representative assigned to that project is unable to adequately address these issues. Each SQA representative assigned to a project should be intimately familiar with the data for his or her project, regardless of who did the actual data base analysis. Ideally, each project representative should do the data analysis for that project.

In a management structure which is functional rather than matrix, the SQA manager or senior SQA department representatives should make a report at least monthly to the software functional executive manager, and immediate managers reporting to that executive. This meeting can be quite effectively utilized where SQA and software configuration management both present relevant information, and where other reports are made on an as-required basis. In this way, the proper focus is brought to the proper level of management in a timely manner.

Consistency in data collection and reporting often is a major factor in evaluating the quality of an SQA data report. For the SQA data reporting and analysis, consistency in the way data is collected, measurements are made, and reports are provided can be a significant factor in determining the reports' worth. This is especially true in a non-matrix structure where managers are responsible for more than one program, or where the personnel are moved from project to project where their particular skills are required. Not having to relearn a new software evaluation reporting methodology can be a considerable time-saver, and saving management team's time is essential for good project control.

Objective Evidence Planning

Requirements for the objective evidence which should be retained is also a part of SQA planning. This is especially important where the project is developed under government contract as a prime or subcontractor. The evidence that SQA has done its job is often crucial to acceptance of the product by the customer. Therefore, for each specific test performed, where any evidence can be kept of the task being accomplished, that evidence should be an element of the objective evidence file system.

Particular attention should be given to the SQA procedures manual, the SQEP and the SQA plan to determine if any of these documents state that objective evidence records are retained. These should be included automatically as a part of the objective evidence. If it is felt that such a record is no longer necessary, then the SQA procedure, SQEP or SQA plan should be changed. If this change is made during the course of a contract, especially a government contract, the change has to be approved by the customer. The provisions of DoD-STD-2167 specifically require that any change to the SQEP be customer-approved. What was originally in the SQA procedures and SQEP became contractually binding, and not following the provisions of these documents means that the contractor is not in contract compliance. An audit by a qualified government auditor will likely result in a quality deficiency report requiring correction to the condition, as well as a plan to assure the condition does not recur.

Objective evidence includes records related to the contract-delivered products, or interim deliveries. This will require some form of SQA identification on the products, and the controlled storage of certain items. Identification can be accomplished by affixing any acceptable stamp or sticker to a document or a computer program media. Identification methods may include provision for a name or initial of the SQA representative, part number of the item, and date. The document or media itself should be clearly labeled as to content.

For computer program media, the master copy of the software should be resident in a controlled library, and only copies of the media should be released by SQA, not the original master copy. If multiple copies are made, the copies should be made serially, each copied from the previous copy, and the final copy compared back to the SQA master copy. If the final copy compares exactly to the SQA bonded master, then the SQA representative can safely affix an SQA sticker (generically referred to hereafter as bonding) to each copy certifying it as a true copy of the master. Naturally, once the copies leave the SQA controlled area, the integrity of any copy can be challenged. If the copy is challenged, it always can be compared to the master again.

Each record of a software media being bonded by SQA, whether a master or a copy, should become part of the SQA objective evidence and a record of the bonding retained by SQA. For tapes and diskettes a data base should be maintained of all media bonded by SQA. It should include the location of the media and identify whether it is a master or copy.

The location identification does not necessarily mean a physical location. It can mean the person to whom the copy was given. For each media distributed, the name of the person and the date should be recorded. If returned, this information should also be recorded, and the media identified as being located within the SQA controlled area.

This controlled area does not have to be controlled by, or manned by, SQA personnel. That is a possibility, of course, but this area also can be manned and controlled by a different department having such an identified responsibility. For example, a department responsible for the maintenance of engineering records, such as drawings, can also be the control point for the software media.

Clearly, if any software media copying is done, the agency making the copy also must have independent integrity from the software developers and test personnel. The chain of control of the master copy of the software media should be comparable to the chain of control of physical evidence in a criminal investigation. It should be unbroken and provide no possibility of tampering.

Objective evidence of document reviews can be accomplished by the SQA representative completing a document review record indicating the document title and revision number, the date reviewed, a summary of any problems, and an indication of whether it was accepted.

Objective evidence of evaluation data, or other SQA data such as inspection data, can be accomplished by having the SQA representative affix a quality control stamp on the document before it is filed. Likewise, SQA reports which result from the data analysis can identify each source document which was included in the material analyzed for the report. Alternatively, the source reports may be retained by SQA, but not identified individually in the evaluation report. Each source report may be initialed or stamped by SQA before filing to ensure the report has been included in the data. The file clerk will then know not to file any report which has not been so identified.

Government-furnished property, usually identified as GFE or GFI (for "equipment" or "information"), is a special category of material and a record of the disposition and control of such property must be kept separately identifiable for each GFE or GFI item under SQA control. If released to another individual, that individual must sign for the item and the transfer record retained in the SQA files. A separate data base file or category should be kept for all government property. Alternatively, there should be a means to sort the regular SQA data base for identification of all government property. Mingling government property information in the same data base as internal property records should be done with great care.

The SQA procedures manual must contain clear and understandable instructions on how objective evidence is to be maintained, for what period of time (this is often contractually determined), in what form, and for which topics.

SQA Interfaces

SQA representatives should have a regular and effective interface with every key element of the contractual process. SQA personnel should be well-known to the program manager, software development managers, software engineering managers, configuration management managers, software testing department managers, library control managers, and customers. SQA representatives should be quite familiar with the current status of their programs at all times. This means, especially if they are functioning at level one, that they are seldom in their offices. That is a difficult situation for the SQA manager in evaluating his or her people from the vantage of direct observation, but that is the job's nature. The evaluation of the SQA personnel is accomplished in large measure by frequent contact with the representatives, obtaining status reports from them on their projects, and by contact with the aforementioned managers to determine how effectively they interface with those departments.

Establishment of the interfaces is very important to accomplishment of the SQA mission. Being aware of the actual status of a project requires a combination of different kinds of input information. The information comes from the data evaluation, of course, but also from the understanding of the project's changing nature.

The project will be driven by cost, schedule, technology, and, possibly, politics. For government contracts, different administrations, which can span one project, as well as different budget allocations and changing political climates, can all affect the progress and direction of a project. Maintaining close contact with all levels of personnel is essential for the effective SQA representative to make the kinds of judgments required as the work continues. Any one or more of the situations and conditions just mentioned can have an impact on the software quality evaluation plan (SQEP), and the SQA representative must be sensitive to that possibility. The need to modify an evaluation program plan may be triggered by more than just the resulting data itself.

Audit Planning

SQA audits are an essential part of the SQA process. The audits are performed on the internal company departments as well as on subcontractors. Subcontractor audits will be addressed in Chapter 8. In this chapter the internal audits will be addressed.

It should go without saying that audits must be planned. Unfortunately, this has not always been completely obvious. An audit, by its nature, is a two-sided process. There is an auditor and there is the one audited. Both have to be considered as part of the planning process.

Audits generally fall into two major categories: planned and unplanned. Planned audits are those which are a regular part of the SQA process. They are scheduled at the beginning of the project and carried out periodically during the development process.

Scheduled audits can be set up to occur every fixed number of weeks or months, or they can be set up to occur at specific and identifiable project milestones. Which type scheduled is a function of the nature of the department audited. If a software development department is going through a series of different and identifiable steps, it might best be audited at milestone points, such as the beginning and end of major life cycle phases. If that same department is developing a large system with multiple major components, where each component might be at a different life cycle phase at any particular time, it might best be audited on a frequency basis, perhaps quarterly.

Each situation has to be examined in order to determine the best way to establish an audit program. This initial evaluation of the audit cycle may have to be modified as the project moves through the life cycles, and the SQA representative should be sensitive to the possibility of a change in audit plans.

Since there are always at least two parties to any audit, the planned audits should be discussed and scheduled with the manager of the department which will be audited. Regularly scheduled audits should never be a surprise to those audited. Participants should know what is expected of them, what evidence will be examined, and the basis for any audit evaluation. If there is a checklist, it should be provided ahead of time so the department audited can be as fully prepared as possible. This will save the time of both parties and make the entire process as efficient and as cost-effective as possible. If a significant part of the audit is to be taken up by SQA review of documents, these documents can be extracted from the files in advance by the audited department. SQA can review them without the department personnel having to be present.

Planned audits are not conducted in an attempt to surprise or "zing" the auditee. They are an attempt to verify and validate that the correct activities are being conducted and the proper records of those activities are being kept. Planned audits are not an adversarial activity, but rather an assurance activity.

Ideally, a planned audit will result in no action items, and no requirement for a re-audit. There is no reason why the audited function should not know in advance what the results of a planned audit will be. There should be no process or product requirements known to software quality which are not also known to the software engineers. The software engineers should be able to complete the audit checklist accurately themselves. The word "should" as used in the last three sentences is why software quality conducts the audits and why there are sometimes action items and other types of required activities which result from a planned audit.

Unplanned audits are those performed without warning. Although SQA generally has a right to conduct unscheduled audits at any time, the use of unscheduled audits usually is reserved for those situations where SQA suspects a problem condition. When an unscheduled audit is conducted, SQA should plan for the audit, develop any necessary special checklists, carefully analyze any documentation which might be pertinent, and know specifically what material is to be requested from the audited department.

At the beginning of the unplanned audit, the SQA representative should make contact with the department manager and inform him or her that the audit will take place. This professional courtesy will serve to put the manager on notice that a condition still exists which warrants such action. The unplanned audit should be preceded by identification of a problem condition, bringing the problem to the attention of the individuals responsible (including the department manager).

Appendix E contains some examples of subcontractor SQA audit checklists, part of which includes an audit of the CM responsibilities. There are two types of audit checklists included. One is a detailed audit checklist based on a contractual government standard, and is cross-referenced to the specific individual paragraphs of that standard. This type of audit checklist might be useful during a first audit of a subcontractor, or for a vendor survey. The other checklist is a more generalized, functionally oriented audit checklist which might be used in follow-up audits. Audit checklists of internal company departments can be developed in a similar way.

Software Development Audits

Audits of software development will principally address the software development processes and the requirements as identified in the contractually imposed standards. For example, the software developers on a government contract where DoD-STD-2167 is imposed may be constrained to use only a high order language (HOL) unless the customer authorizes otherwise. The developers also may be constrained to use only specific constructs, such as IF. . .THEN, DO. . .WHILE, CASE, and the like. There may also be constraints on the use of recursivity in programming, and prohibition of certain instructions, such as the GO-TO. Determining what these conditions are is a part of the initial quality planning.

The audit will involve the determination of whether there are any deviations from these conditions, and the determination of whether permission has been given by the customer waiving one or more of the standards requirements.

The time required to assess these conditions can vary considerably depending on the availability of automated tools to assist the auditor. The time required in performing a manual assessment by looking through listings can be an almost impossible task on a large project unless only a small sample is examined. Performing an audit requiring manual examination of code listings on a large program having many modules totalling hundreds of thousands of executable lines of code, or more, can take weeks or months, and may require that the SQA representative(s) be quite conversant with the particular language employed. If several languages are employed on the particular project, the task may be impossible to do manually. How this might affect the contractual requirement to do so, and to certify (required by DoD-STD-2167) to the customer that the conditions have not been violated, should be of serious concern to the SQA manager and the program manager. Clearly, ignoring the requirement is not the answer.

If automated source code analysis tools are used, the possibility exists for the SQA representative to accomplish the task and do so on 100 percent of the product. However, the programmers can utilize such tools most effectively by exercising them on the code as it is being developed or modified. Under this situation SQA can use the automated tool on a random set of software, or even just audit the results obtained by the programmer. In any case, SQA should not utilize automated tools on the code to which the programmers themselves do not have access.

For example, using Logiscope[3], the SQA representative can invoke the control graph option and look at a picture of the module (Figure 3.1). In Figure 3.1, different constructs which might be employed in a module are displayed. A composite of the different constructs results in a picture of the entire module (Figure 3.2). The logic flow is displayed graphically and the result is what you might call an X-ray of the program. It will not describe the function of the module, but will display the logic flow of the module. By following the arrows, the programmer or

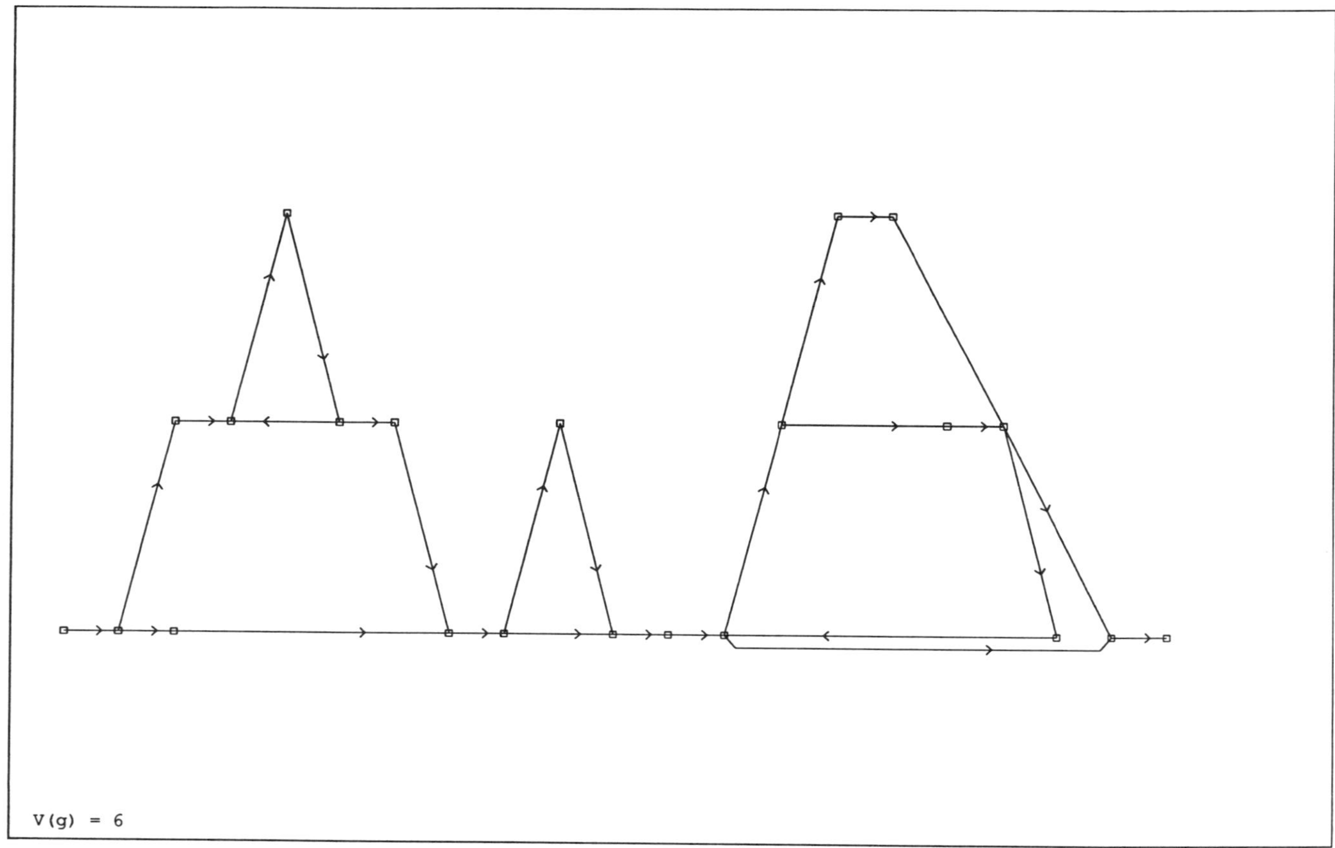

Figure 3.1 Control Graph Option Results in Module Picture

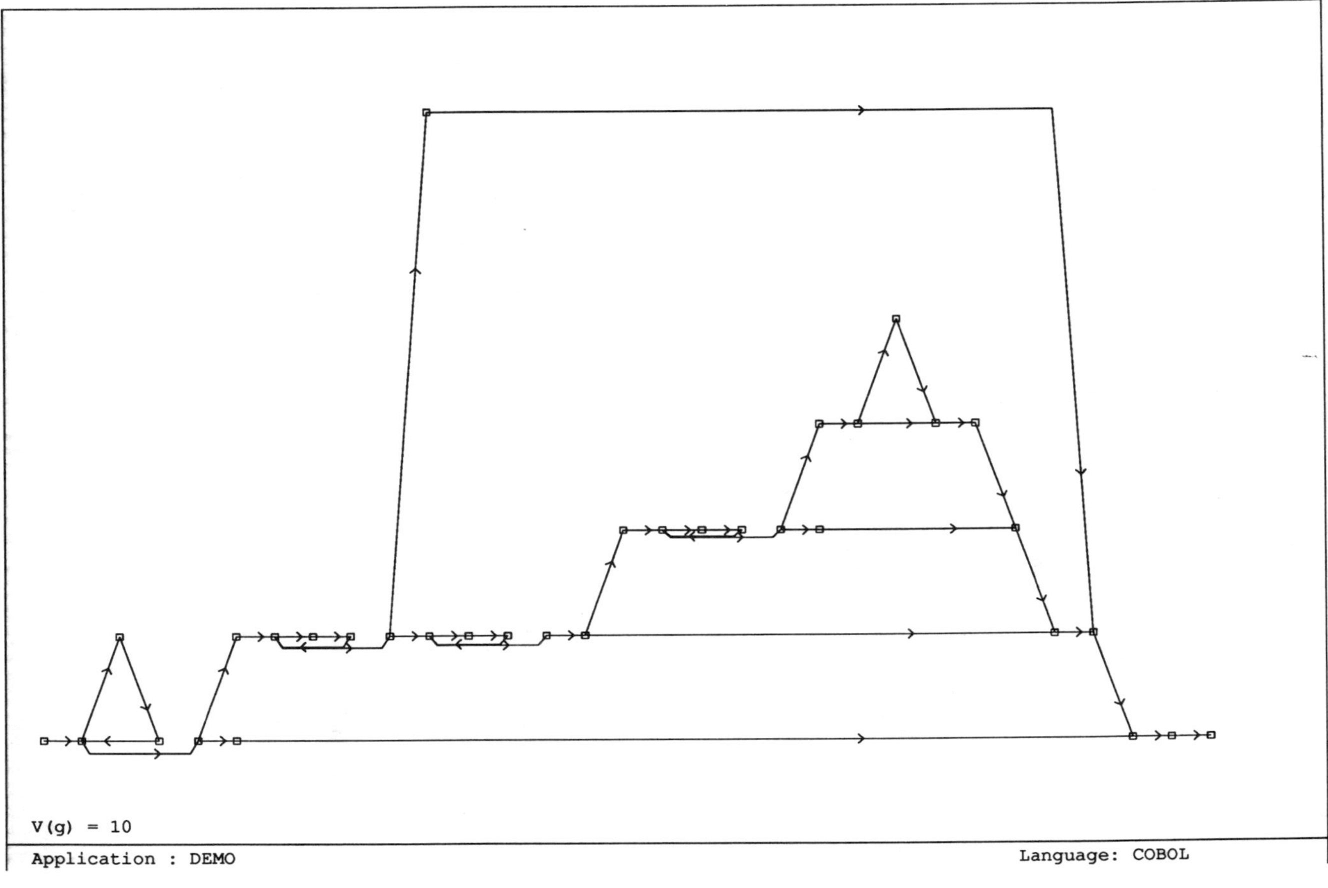

Figure 3.2 Composite of Different Constructs Displays Entire Module

SQA representative can determine whether there are any GO-TOs in the program, what the program constructs are, whether there are any extraneous entry or exit points in the program, how well-structured the module is, whether there is any inaccessible code, and the module cyclomatic complexity.

The graphic output eliminates the need for an in-depth knowledge of the language itself, and the automated analysis can provide results for any one, or any group of modules in the system. In this way, the SQA representative has ready access to the automated analysis results for 100 percent of the programs, and this data can become part of the SQA archive files, or, conversely, part of the programmers' files audited by SQA.

Most importantly, since Logiscope can be implemented on a mainframe, the programmers can access this tool directly to assist themselves in controlling their software development. Thus, they assure themselves that their modules always obey the rules for constructs, are always well-structured, and have a manageable level of complexity. Printout of the graphic output can be included in the programmer's notebook for each module. Since the programmers would have direct access to this analysis tool, there is no need for them to worry about someone else finding any problems which may have been created. They can find their own problems first, and correct them immediately.

During the development process, since Logiscope has an archive capability, the data associated with each module can be archived by module name and version number, thereby providing a pictorial history of the module's development as it changes over time. For example, the data in Figures 3.3, 3.4, and 3.5, shows the progressive history of the changes made to a module. As is obviously seen, the module is deteriorating rather than improving, finally resulting in a condition where an entire section of the module is inaccessible (usually referred to as dead code).

Figure 3.6 shows a condition where the module is not at all well-structured, has multiple entry points, and several GO-TOs. Figure 3.7 shows a typical example of what can happen when a module is rushed into code without adequate design time. There are extraneous entry points, the module structure is very poor, and, on further analysis, it was shown that the entire top half of the module was unnecessary. The final result was the elimination of the top half altogether, thereby resulting in a module which was much less complex, and had about half the previous number of test paths, half the throughput time, much better structure, better capability of being documented and maintained, and one which could be tested in a reasonable manner.

Figure 3.8 shows a module which is virtually beyond hope. It is clearly not maintainable, is not documentable, is very poorly

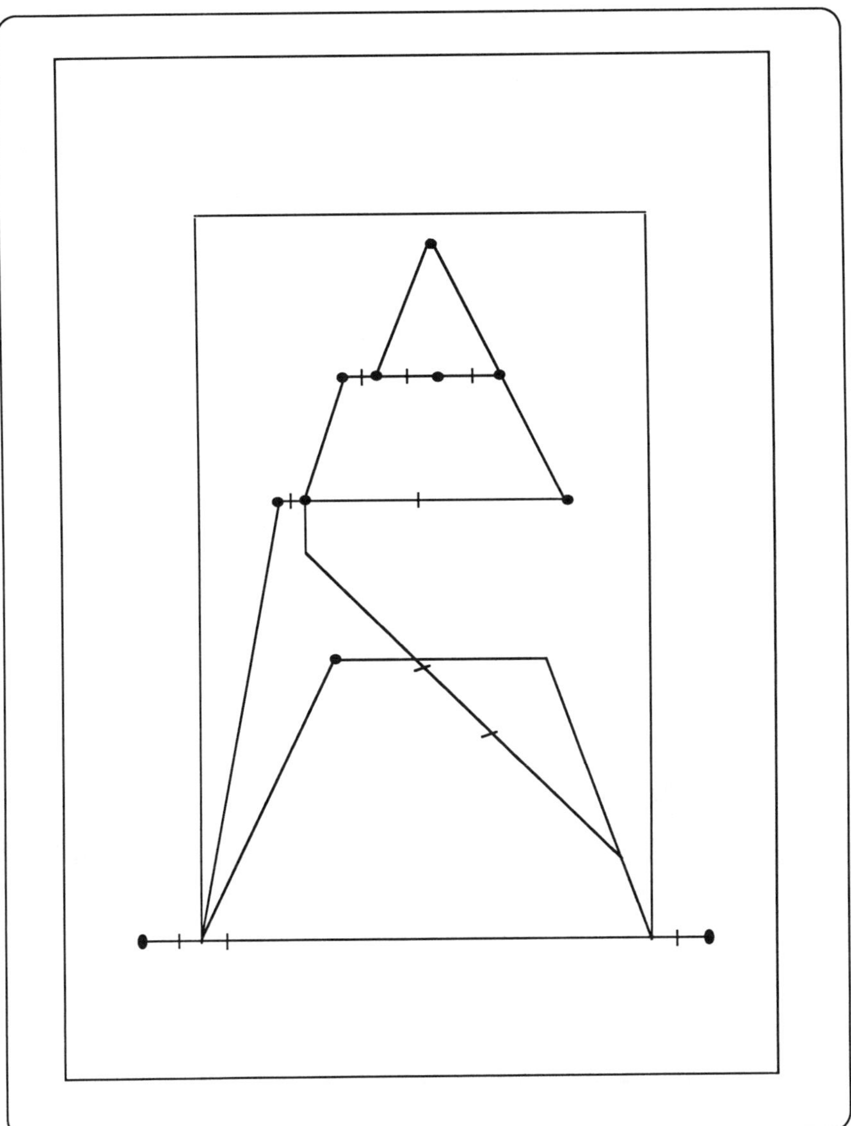

Figure 3.3 Stage One of Changes Made to a Module

structured, and is unacceptably complex. No responsible developer should ever deliver such a module to a customer.

The developers, having access to such data during the development and test phases, can control their programs' structure and never get involved in the types of conditions which have been illustrated in some of the previous examples.

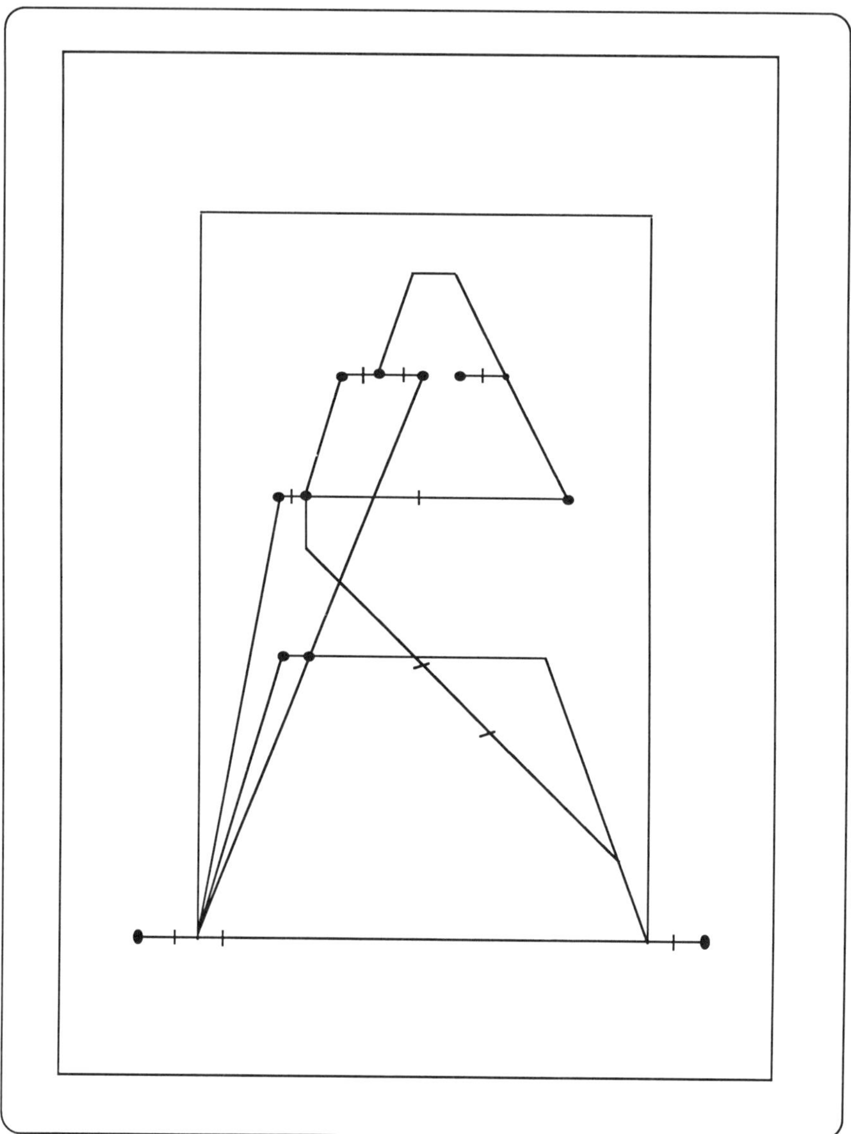

Figure 3.4 Module Starts to Deteriorate

Configuration Management Audit

The configuration management (CM) department is audited by SQA according to the life cycle activity points reflecting the times when deliverable items are placed under configuration control, or when configuration milestone events occur. This includes creation of the specification tree, initiation of SCCB activity, or, later in development, when the physical configuration

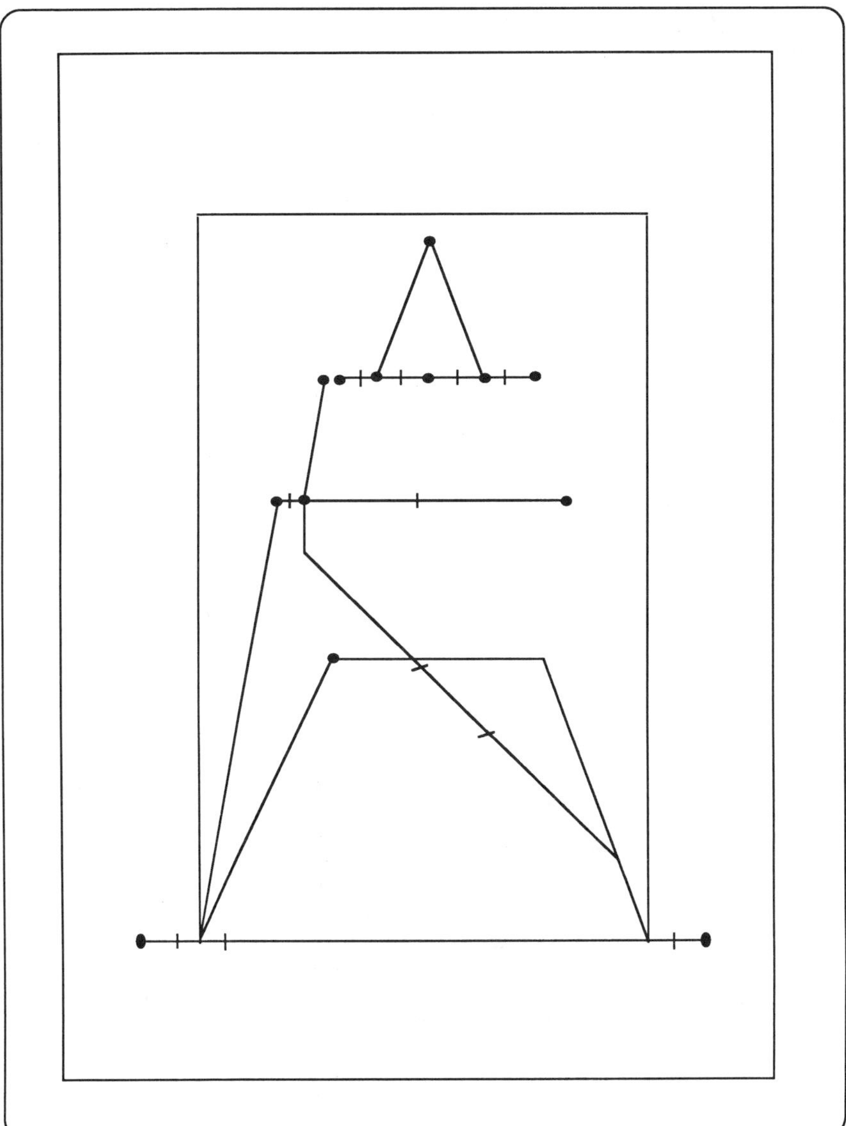

Figure 3.5 Module Continues to Deteriorate

audit (PCA) and functional configuration audit (FCA) occur. These events may be specified by the contractual standards specifying that certain tasks be done. These same standards also specify that SQA is responsible for certifying that all of the standards' provisions are followed.

In performing the audit, SQA must understand the difference between configuration management and configuration control. Configuration control can be accomplished by any of several

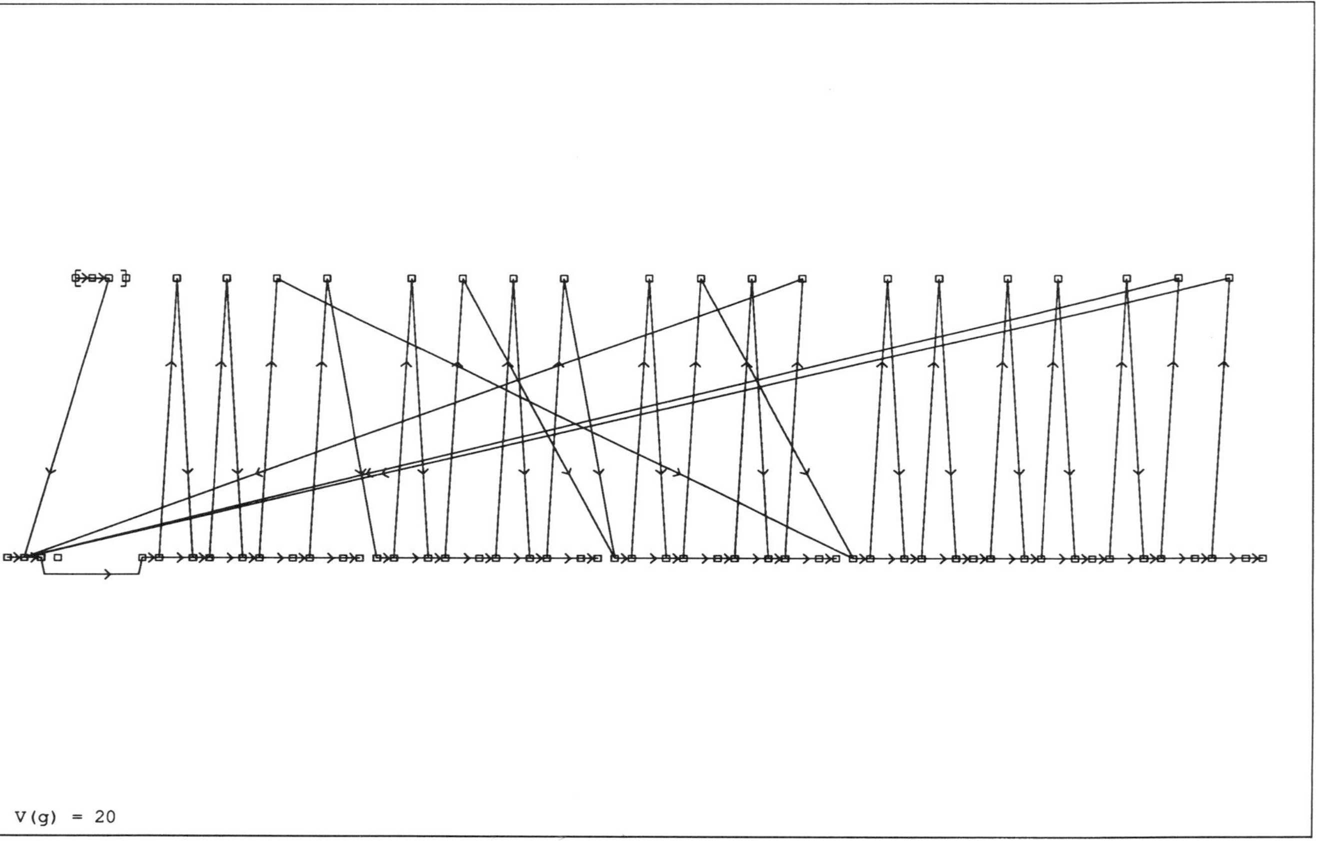

Figure 3.6 A Poorly Structured Module with Multiple Entry Points and Several GO-TOs

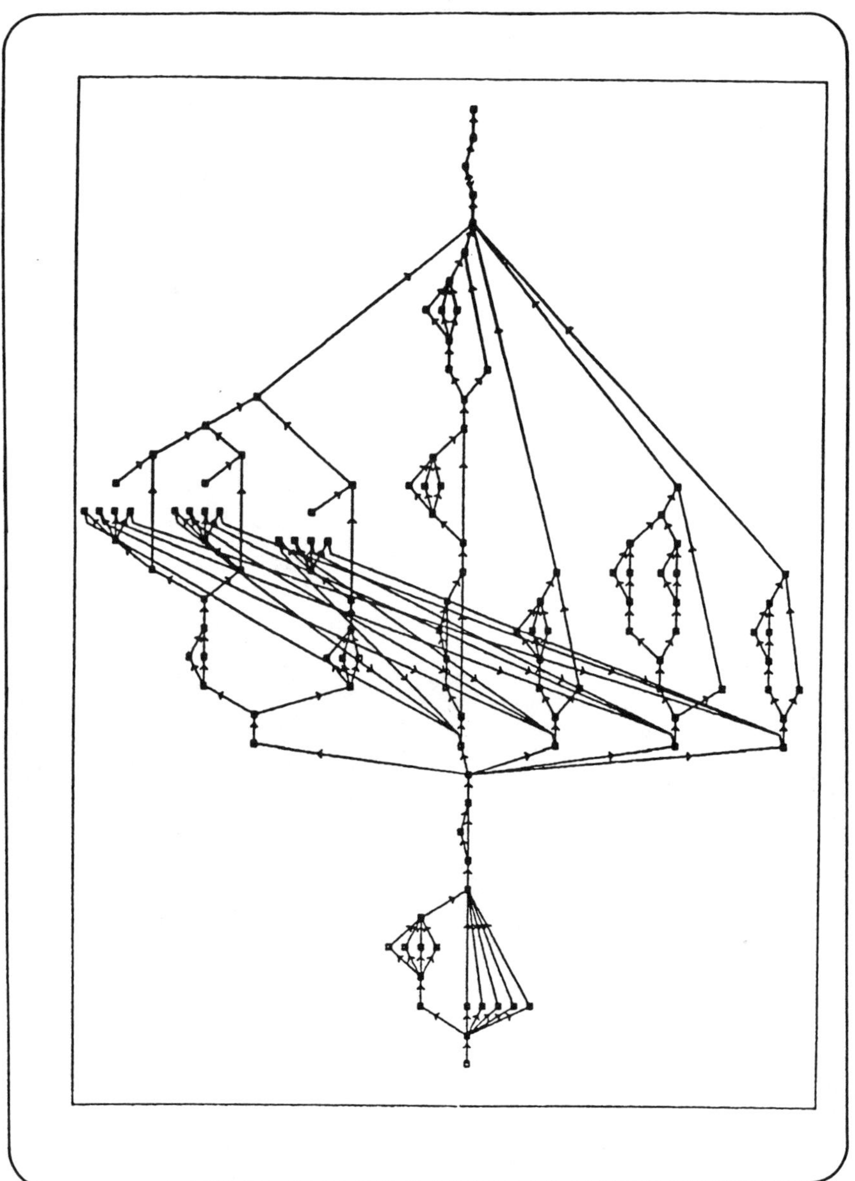

Figure 3.7 Inadequately Designed Module

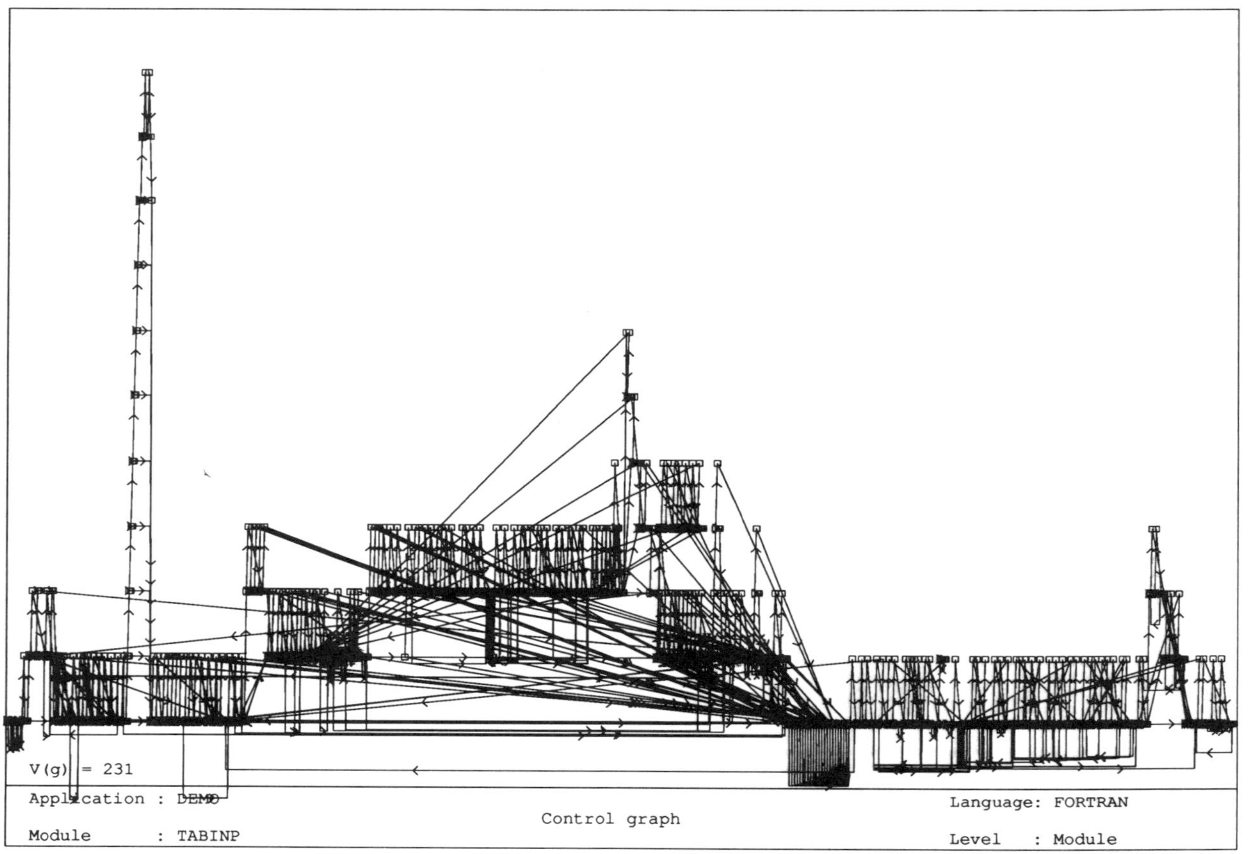

Figure 3.8 Completely Unacceptable Module

departments (preferably not software development, test or engineering), including SQA. This function fundamentally involves the performance of system builds and maintenance of the controlled libraries. In some companies, a separate software configuration control department is established.

Configuration management (CM) functions are more concerned with the proper management and control of the software system configuration and establishment of documentation trees. Often, a CM person serves as the chairperson of the software configuration control board (SCCB). The CM functions are usually well-identified on government contracts, the responsibilities being specified in the government standards imposed on the contract. For example, one function usually included in the CM responsibilities is the requirement to assure that each line of executable code exactly matches the documentation for that code. (See DoD-STD-1679A and DoD-STD-2167A, par 4.5.1d-f.)

When performing an audit of CM, the SQA representative must clearly identify the CM responsibilities as defined in the contractual standards and in the software CM plan for that project. An audit checklist should be created and used during the audit's conduct. As is the case with all audits, an audit report is produced following the audit and retained as a part of the SQA objective evidence file. Also included in the process is a debrief of the audit results with the Software CM manager.

Library Control Audit

An SQA audit of the library control function is essential to assure that the controlled library system has adequate protection against unauthorized modification. It also is essential to assure that, when system builds are done, the correct configurations (all necessary modules, and only the correct modules, are included and the correct version of each is included) are known and incorporated into the build. It also is very desirable that the system build process be automated to the maximum extent possible, even though this is not an absolute requirement in the government standards. It also is very desirable that the system be able to offer control down to the individual line of source code.

One of the best commercial automated tools developed so far is the CCC^4 tool developed by SOFTOOL Corporation.

Change and configuration control environment (CCC) is a SOFTOOL Corporation automated, integrated software configuration control and configuration management tool. CCC is fully commensurate with the provisions of DoD-STD-2167, as well as other pertinent military and DoD standards and specifications.

The CCC environment specifically meets the needs for software change control, configuration control, and status accounting. CCC provides the following general capabilities:

1. Configuration management and control and status accounting for both baseline development and baselines.

2. Explicit management controls and visibility into ongoing software code change status.

3. Software library usage and control functions applicable to documentation, PDL, and source and object code.

4. Programmer relief from tedious and error-prone documentation tasks.

5. Minimization of storage requirements by automatically exploiting the commonality between different versions of software documentation and code.

6. Effective, and easy use, with minimal training, for both managers and programmers.

7. Availability across a wide number of different computers.

CCC provides capabilities that support its immediate application to the development and control of software in a military standard environment. These capabilities are summarized as follows:

1. CM control and status accounting

   a. All DoD standards dealing with configuration management, such as DoD-STD-1679A section 5.11, DoD-STD-2167 paragraph 5.7, and MIL-STD-483A, require that developers maintain control over software configurations and change processing. A major concern in the development community involves maintaining such control and ensuring the accuracy of status accounting reports.

   b. CCC meets this challenge through a combination of its library control functions and its numerous reporting capabilities. CCC can keep a record of every change ever made by a user. Thus, CCC is capable of reconstructing any unit (e.g., source code, document, testing procedure) as it was at any point in time (e.g., "Reconstruct my program to the way it was on January 23, 1986, at 2:00 a.m."). This capability is of utmost importance for it ensures contractor compliance with the MIL-standard requirements for development traceability, and the requirements for the effective and successful conduct of a PCA. Additionally, CCC provides the ability to create any number of configurations, in accordance with DoD-STD-2167 paragraph 5.7.1, to specify who has access to each configuration, to combine and delete configurations, and to obtain reports which pinpoint differences between configuration components.

c. Use of this capability by any software developer would be of significant value in achieving the many goals of government contracts, and commercial in-house development, related to maintainability and configuration control, especially where the maintenance activity is responsible for multiple versions of a software product. The CCC simplified version control provides the means for keeping track of changes that occur to individual versions, and provides the information necessary to quickly determine site differences.

d. When changes are made to the software, CCC provides the means to easily identify both the responsible individual and the exact change made. It can also pinpoint the exact date and time the change was made. These capabilities provide an excellent tool for contractor use in the period between government-sanctioned baselines, when internal control is critical. Additionally, differences between various versions of software can be identified quickly, allowing continuous accurate reporting of configuration status.

2. Management control and visibility

a. All military standards dealing with software development, configuration management, and engineering management require that developers plan, organize, direct, control, and coordinate defense systems software development and procedures in a manner which provides an acceptable level of development visibility into the development process both to the project management and to the end user or procuring agency.

b. CCC provides some capabilities which allow specification of:

1. How information is to be stored and organized

2. Who has access and the type of access

3. What type of status and control information

c. These capabilities provide a means for fulfilling MIL-standard development control and visibility requirements while not inhibiting the development process.

3. Library usage and control

a. The military standard software development requirements, as well as good development practice, dictate that some form of library and usage control be employed. Use of automated functions provides an efficient process for library control and minimizes the personnel requirements necessary for library maintenance.

b. CCC provides excellent facilities for meeting program support library requirements. The capability to easily yet rigidly control library read and write access, combined with the ability to rapidly review any changes that are made, simultaneously ensures both that a central repository of information is maintained for immediate access (read-only) and control (read-write). Additionally, CCC provides the ability to quickly reconstruct software versions which existed at any point in time, so that changes do not permanently alter the library.

4. Security

a. Software development and maintenance in the DoD environment requires the ability to enforce appropriate access controls easily and smoothly. These needs are often not met by the facilities offered by computer operating systems. CCC offers a powerful and flexible protection mechanism that addresses the DoD needs directly.

5. Integrity

   a. Software development and maintenance in the military standard environment requires that the integrity of the information be assured. CCC supports this need fully and automatically.

6. Storage minimization

   a. Software development in the military contract environment must be planned to minimize software life cycle costs while maximizing software reliability and maintainability factors. CCC, while providing sound development/maintenance support, also minimizes software storage requirements. By providing the ability to reconstruct individual versions from component units, CCC requires only one copy of each unit (where a unit can be any part of the product down to a single line of code) which is common to two or more versions to be retained. Thus, both development and maintenance support requirements can be minimized.

   b. This capability greatly enhances the maintenance task since multiple versions are consolidated into a space only slightly larger than that required for one version. Thus, many or even all versions may be readily accessible without the need for multiple tape/disk loading, filing, and tracking.

Although the features of CCC have been described in terms of their meeting the government requirements, it should be clear that all of these features are desirable in any library control system, government contractor or not. The SQA audit of a library control system should focus on the degree to which that system provides the kind of control facilities as described.

Audit Reports

Following every audit, SQA should file an audit report. This report should identify the function audited, a copy of the audit checklist filled in, a summary of significant findings, and the list of any action items resulting from the audit. Therefore, during the SQA planning phase, the audit planning should include planning for the time and effort required to prepare for the audits, perform the audits, and produce the various audit reports. Care should be taken to include this in the SQA budget activity.

Audit reports should be retained in the SQA files as a part of the SQA objective evidence, and also sent to the manager of the department audited, with a copy to the SQA manager and, for nonscheduled audits, the project program manager or others who have a need to know.

Notes

1. Master Planner is a copyright product of SFPS, Inc.

2. McCall, J.A., "The Utility of Software Quality Metrics in Large Scale Software System Developments." General Electric Company, Sunnyvale, California.

3. Logiscope is a copyright product of VERILOG, S. A., Toulouse, France.

4. CCC is a copyright product of SOFTOOL Corporation.

CHAPTER 4

SOFTWARE INSPECTION PROCESS

Introduction

The inspection process was first introduced by Michael Fagan[1] in 1976. Since then it has been implemented in several large companies with excellent results. The intent of this chapter is to describe the implementation of the inspection process as it is applied during the design and code phases.

Design and code inspections are very cost-effective and a marked departure from other similarly intentioned processes, such as reviews and walk-throughs. Inspections are characterized by formality, rigor, consistency, scheduling, phasing, and associated documentation (i.e., imposed and measurable self-discipline). Inspections particularly address the need for a *manageable* software development process, and one for which the input, output, and internal processes are well described. It also satisfies the need for a process, or series of process steps, for which there is an entry and exit criterion at each phase. This removes ambiguity and allows high visibility through the establishment of definitive process control checkpoints. The establishment of these process control checkpoints requires the collection, analysis and dissemination of data essential to the exercise of the management control function.

Utilizing only this inspection process, as many as 70 percent of the software life-cycle defects have been effectively and regularly removed *prior* to the first software test, without using other costly computer and manpower resources. Because of this achievement, this inspection process utilization has been extended to the requirements phase, thereby increasing the impact and scope of benefits to be derived from inspections.

When inspections are used in combination with automated source code analyzers, such as Logiscope, the result will be high quality, highly reliable, and easily maintained software, developed in an environment providing the management team with the visibility required for effective technical and cost control.

The inspection process is most effectively implemented where the software management and development personnel are trained in both the mechanics of the process as well as the psychology related to inspections. Both are essential.

Definitions

The following definitions are applicable to this chapter's contents.

a. Inspection—A formal, rigorous examination of a software product by a small group of peers of the author of that product.
b. Peer—A person who is a professional co-worker of the author of a software product (design or code), and who works on the same task or contract as the author, and is either in the software development, systems engineering or software test organization.
c. Moderator—The moderator is part of the inspection team and is responsible for the successful completion of all six phases of the inspection process. The moderator serves as the manager of that particular inspection. The moderator should be a more senior member of the inspection team.
d. Inspector—All of the members of the inspection team, including the author and moderator.
e. Reader—The reader is any of the inspectors other than the moderator or author. The reader "reads" the material, by paraphrasing or other means, during the inspection meeting.
f. Preparation time—The amount of time each inspector spent preparing for the inspection meeting. This does not include time spent by the author to develop the design or code.
g. Inspection time—The amount of time spent by each team member at the inspection meeting.
h. Inspection meeting—The time during which the inspection team members, after sufficient preparation, meet to discuss the defects in the software product.
i. Follow-up—The period of time during which the moderator verifies that the noted defects are corrected.
j. Inspection defect log—That form on which the individual inspectors record defects found during the preparation time period.
k. Design/code inspection summary—That form on which the moderator summarizes the results of the inspection meeting.

l. Rework—That activity engaged in by the author to correct the defects listed on the summary defect log and to verify the correctness of the change.

m. Re-inspection—A re-inspection is the re-examination of the software product, using the same process as the original inspection. The moderator makes the decision as to whether or not to re-inspect. Re-inspection generally is required if more than 5 percent of the software product must be changed to correct the deficiencies identified, or if the defects require complex corrections, or if the requirements have changed significantly.

Purposes of the Inspection

There are both primary and secondary purposes for conducting these inspections. The primary vs. secondary categorization has more to do with the process of conducting the inspections than the net impact of having done inspections. The inspection process training and conduct emphasizes that there are important, definable, secondary purposes which are achieved as a by-product of properly conducted inspections, and are benefits not previously defined or achieved through other similar processes.

Primary Purpose

The inspection, whether design or code, has only one primary purpose: to remove defects as early as possible in the development process. The purpose of the inspection preparation and meeting is to:

- Identify potential defects during preparation and validate them at the inspection meeting.

- Validate whether or not the identified items are actual defects.

- Record the existence of the defect.

- Provide a record to the developer to use in making fixes.

- Provide a means for the discovery of additional defects as a result of interaction during the inspection meeting.

Secondary Purposes

There are secondary purposes which result from the inspection process. These are:

- Provide traceability of requirements to design.
- Provide a technically correct base for the next phase of development.
- Increase programming process quality.
- Increase software product quality at delivery.
- Lower life cycle cost.
- Increase effectiveness of test activity.
- Provide a first indication of program maintainability.
- Encouragement of entry/exit criteria software management.

These secondary purposes are all part of the net effect of performing inspections properly and professionally. The fact that they are secondary purposes does not in any way diminish their importance to the overall software development effort.

If the inspections are performed properly, then these secondary benefits will be achieved.

Inspection Phases

The moderator of an inspection is responsible for the entire inspection process for that software product. There are six distinct inspection phases. They are: planning, overview, preparation, inspection meeting, rework, and follow-up.

Planning

The planning phase is that phase during which the moderator establishes the conduct and progress for the entire inspection. This requires that the moderator assure the identification of the inspection team, assure that the team members will be able to adequately prepare for the inspection, assure that the materials to be inspected are available and conform to standards, determine if the entry criteria have been met, determine the need for an overview, assure that the place for the inspection meeting is available and reserved for the inspection, schedule the inspection meeting time and place, and give all inspection team members and other interested parties notice of the inspection meeting time and place.

Some of these tasks may be accomplished by someone other than the moderator, and often the author will schedule the meeting place, pass out the materials, and other such tasks. However, it is still the responsibility of the moderator to assure that these tasks are accomplished.

Overview

An overview meeting is an educational meeting usually conducted prior to a design inspection. It is a short meeting where the author of the product to be inspected gives the inspection team members, and others who will be interfacing with the author's product, a brief description of the software, what task is being performed, how it will perform that task, what interfaces are to be active, and a description of the interface functions. Such a meeting provides insight to the inspection team members and makes their job easier. It also provides other programmers who will interface with the program being inspected an opportunity to learn how the interface will be handled and, if necessary, identify any problems with the described approach. If there are any significant problems, the inspection can be postponed and the problems addressed.

The overview meeting is held at the beginning of the preparation phase and it is here that the moderator gives the inspection materials and inspection meeting notice to inspection team members. Otherwise, the moderator assures the materials are distributed to team members at the beginning of the preparation phase. The moderator may not do the actual distribution, but he/she does have the responsibility to assure the distribution is made.

Whether there is an overview meeting held or not is discretionary with the moderator. This is the only discretionary phase.

Preparation

The preparation phase begins when inspection team members receive the inspection materials and notice of the inspection meeting. Everything needed for the inspection is provided to the inspectors at one time. The inspectors receive these materials at least five working days in advance of the inspection meeting. This lead time is to give inspectors the opportunity to properly examine the materials and record any discrepancies found. Since each inspector has other responsibilities, the lead time is to allow them to perform their assigned tasks and to prepare for the inspection meeting. It is expected that inspection team members will spend at least as much time preparing for the inspection as is required for the inspection meeting. Inspection meetings should not exceed two hours.

During this time, the reader prepares to present the material to the inspection team. The reader makes particular note of any difficulty in understanding the design, code, or commentary. Each inspector examines the material for all possible defects. Defects are recorded on the inspection defect log, which is included in the inspection materials provided by the moderator. Each inspector also keeps track of and records the preparation time on the inspection defect log.

Inspection Meeting

The inspection meeting is that phase of the inspection process where team members come together to discuss the discrepancies which have been detected. The moderator is responsible for the proper conduct of the meeting and for assuring that the team members approach this task in a professional manner. The reader is responsible for presenting the product to the team in a logical and orderly manner so that discussion of the material, and any inherent defects, is not hindered.

During this phase, the moderator calls the meeting to order, records the preparation time for each team member, and directs the reader to begin the discussion.

As defects are identified, they are discussed in a professional manner and recorded. Particular attention is paid to the detection of previously unidentified defects which are discovered as a result of the discussion and interaction between team members. Also important is the verification that items identified for discussion are true defects. The defects are then recorded, the defect type is noted, and, at the end of the inspection meeting, the defects are counted and categorized by the moderator.

The activity during the meeting is limited to finding defects, not solutions. It is the responsibility of the author to find the solutions. If a defect is a type which repeats itself, the team need discuss it only once. When summarizing the defects, the moderator counts the defect once for each occurrence.

When the inspection meeting is over, the moderator collects the individual defect logs from the team. If the moderator is able to tell from the result of the meeting that a re-inspection will or will not be required, it is announced then. If the defects will have to be examined first, then the moderator should do this in a timely manner.

When the inspection team has been dismissed, the moderator summarizes the defects found on the defect summary log, records the preparation and inspection time, notes the author, department (or subcontractor company name), notes the requirement for a re-inspection, notes whether or not this inspection was a re-inspection, notes the type of inspection, and sends a copy of the data to the author and to the software quality assurance (SQA) department.

Rework

During the rework phase, the author examines the defects found and makes the necessary corrections. After the corrections are verified, the author discusses the corrections with the moderator. If a re-inspection is required, the author begins preparation for the re-inspection.

Follow-Up

The follow-up phase is that activity engaged in by the moderator to assure that all defects detected during the inspection have been corrected. The moderator is responsible for the activity in this phase, and the inspection is not terminated until the follow-up phase has been completed by the moderator. Completion of this phase completes the task of the moderator for the inspection.

The moderator has the responsibility to assure that each defect has been corrected. This verification is done in person, not by phone. If necessary, the moderator brings a member of the inspection team to assist in the verification process. The fix date (or the date when the fix was verified) is noted on a copy of the defect log. When this is completed, the moderator sends a copy of the summary log to software quality assurance (SQA) with the notation that this is a fix notification. When this task is complete, the moderator's task for this inspection is complete.

When the follow-up phase is completed, so is the inspection for that software product. Complete data results are entered into the data base maintained by SQA. It is from this data base that the inspection data reports are provided. Examples of the types of data reported are included in the following discussion.

Design and Code Inspection Types

There are three inspection types typically performed. These are: the high-level design inspection (I_0), performed to provide the high-level design phase exit criteria necessary to begin low-level design; the low-level design inspection (I_1), performed to provide the exit criteria necessary to begin the code phase; and the code inspection (I_2), performed to provide the exit criteria necessary to begin unit test.

High-Level Design Inspection (I_0)

The high-level design phase is that phase during which the overall design for a module or function is produced. This stage commences with issuance of a preliminary program performance specification (PPS), the initiation of the interface design specification (IDS), and concludes with completion of the I_0 inspection. In this stage, the high-level architecture of the software is determined and recorded in the initial program design specification (PDS) material. This PDS information is examined during the I_0 inspection. For each function, the PDS will provide:

1. The source of the design (new, other contract, etc.).
2. A graphical presentation of the function allocation to hardware resources.
3. A graphical presentation of function flow.
4. A description of scheduling, timing, and synchronization.
5. A definition of interfaces.
6. The process of decomposition.
7. The design definition:
    - Retained modules: reference to an existing PDS, if applicable.
    - Modified modules: reference to an existing PDS, where applicable, and a narrative description of the changes.
    - New modules: high-level description of the interfaces and processing.

During the I_0, the PDS information is further expanded to include a description of each new task/module, including interfacing and processing. An I_0 is held for each function.

For the retained and modified modules, an inspection plan is written by the programmer which defines the required further level of inspection. These requirements are based on the anticipated extent of modification.

Resource utilization estimates are generated during this design phase and are collected and maintained by system engineering, which developed the PPS, with software development periodically providing input. The system engineering organization reviews and approves the PDS and I_0 material to assure compliance with the baseline documentation.

All six phases of the inspection process (with the possible exception of the overview phase) are conducted for each I_0.

Purpose of the High-Level Design Inspection (I_0)

The unique purpose of the I_0 inspection, in addition to finding defects, is to conduct a formal examination of the software product to verify that the functional design at the task level is a correct expansion of the PPS at the mode level. A mode level function may be any major self-contained function of the software, including, navigation, fire control, telemetry processing, etc. The verification is performed by identifying the allocation of PPS requirements to processes and tasks. A single I_0 is typically performed for each mode.

I_0 Data Analysis

Examples, taken from an actual program, of the types of data analysis graphics output available to management as a result of the application of the I_0 inspection process include, but are not limited to, the following (note that for this particular project, the software volume in January was approximately 100,000 lines, and in September it was almost 1,000,000 lines):

1. Defect percentages: The major defects detected, and removed, during the I_0 inspections are shown by defect type, as a percentage of the total major defects detected. A major defect is one which would result in a program trouble report (PTR) being written if it is found during software or system test. This is the pie chart shown as Figure 4.1.

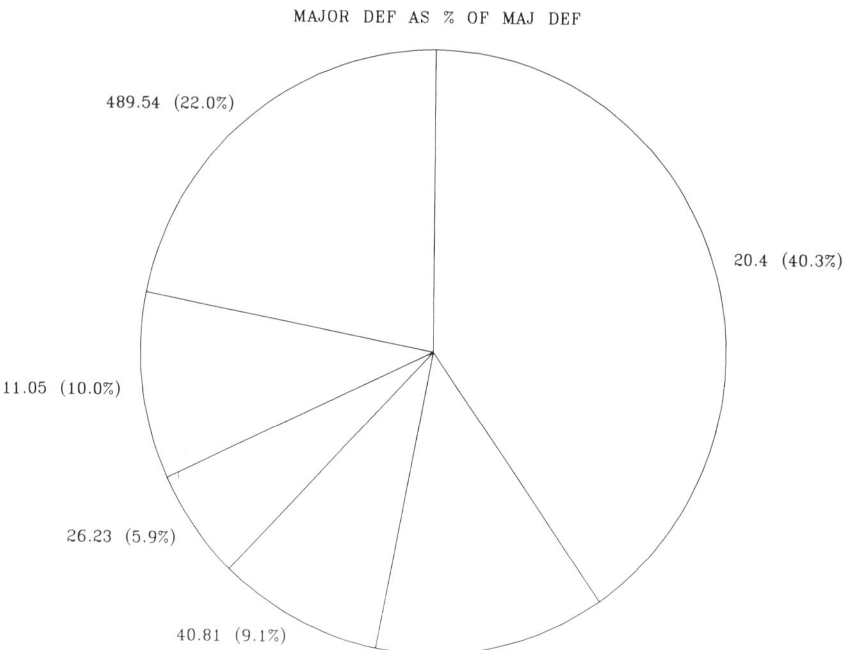

Figure 4.1 Pie Chart of Project B I_0 Inspections

2. Defect totals: The total major defects detected, by defect type. This data corresponds to the percentage data shown in Figure 4.1. This is the bar chart shown as Figure 4.2.

3. Defect density: The total defects, major and minor, detected and removed, per thousand source lines of code (KSLOC), during the I_0 inspections. This is the line chart shown as Figure 4.3.

4. Inspection efficiency: The inspection process effectiveness is shown in summary form by the data in Figures 4.1, 4.2, and 4.3. However, the inspections performed do require a certain level of manpower, and therefore the efficiency of the inspection process also is measured. The efficiency is measured in terms of the total number of manhours expended to conduct the inspection process (not including the time to fix the defects found) per major defect detected. Only major defects are considered for this chart (although all of the manhours are included) so that these cost elements can be legitimately compared to the cost elements for detection

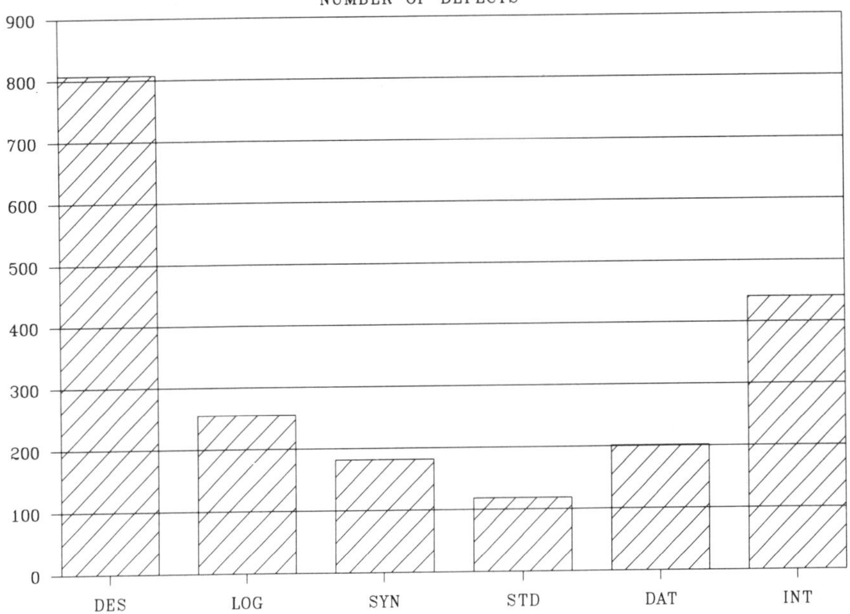

Figure 4.2 Bar Chart of Project B I_0 Total Defects by Type

during the test phases, and the only defects which would be found in test are those which are classified as major. Minor defects include such defects as code commentary errors, which would never be seen in test since the code commentary is not executable. This is shown in Figure 4.4.

5. Individual defect data: Other charts displaying data related to individual defect types (such as the density of design defects over a period of time) are available, but not included here in the interest of saving space.

Low-Level Design Inspection (I_1)

The low-level design, or what is more commonly called detailed or module design, reflects attention on the overall design objectives. Key objectives considered in designing the software are:

1. Accuracy and performance requirements.

2. Reliable and fault-tolerant software, so that the system will continue to perform in the event of hardware intermittent failures or other unexpected occurrences.

Figure 4.3 Line Chart Displaying Defect Density of Project B I_0 Inspections

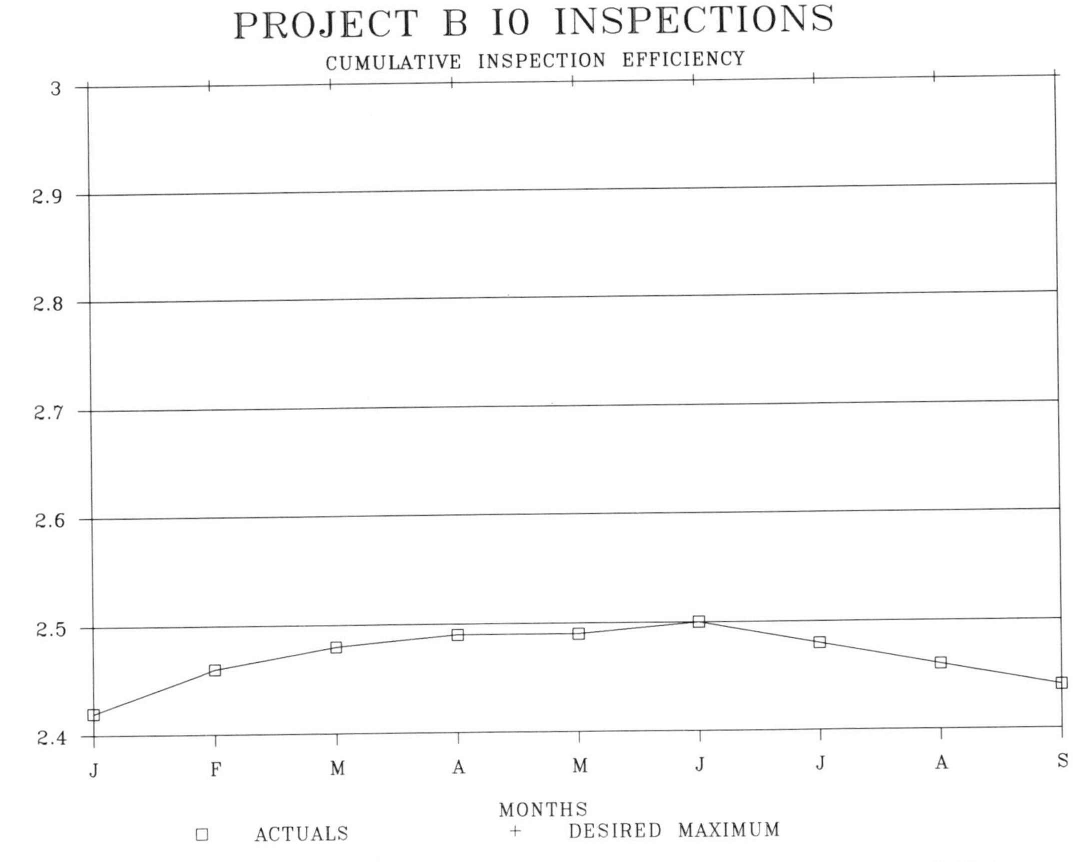

Figure 4.4 Project B I_0 Inspection Measurement of Inspection Process Efficiency

3. The software is flexible and can accommodate change and growth.

4. The software can be tested easily.

5. The software can be maintained easily.

Detail module design is developed and I_1 inspections are held for all modules which meet any of the following criteria:

1. New module development.

2. Any change to the external interface or function of an existing module.

3. A structural change in an existing module.

4. A 40 percent or greater change in the source lines of code (SLOC) in an existing module. This percentage presumes that the size requirements as specified in the military standards are adhered to. In the case of unrestricted module size, where the module is large, this percentage criterion is re-evaluated.

To improve maintainability, each new module, member, or subroutine process is documented within itself (the documentation is created as part of the software module source code listing) as follows:

1. It contains a prologue, or preamble, which describes the routine function, inputs, outputs, revision levels, and process flow. The detailed requirements for such a prologue are found in MIL-STD-1679, paragraph 5.4.4.1, and will apply on all contracts on which this standard has been imposed.

2. Comments for each section are blocked and, in turn, the blocked comments delineate the routine into logical segments and describe the function of each segment.

3. Inline comments clarify specific statements. There are inline comment requirements also specified in MIL-STD-1679, paragraph 5.4.4.2.

Purpose of the Low-Level Design Inspection (I_1)

The unique objective of the I_1, in addition to finding defects, is to stepwise refine the I_0 design to an intermediate level before translation to the target language code is authorized. All interfaces between processes, tasks and procedures are defined to the field or bit level. The level of decomposition must be sufficient to show the highest level of control structure for each procedure and show the operations performed on the inputs and outputs. All the control structures and all the internal data structures, if not completely defined during the low-level design, will be completed during the code phase.

All six phases of the inspection process (with the possible exception of the overview phase) are conducted for each I_1.

Only after the successful completion of the I_1 inspection, and any required re-inspections, can the module coding process begin. Managers have the responsibility to assure that no code begins on a module until successful completion of the design inspection for that module. This is a technical and product quality decision and should not be controlled by schedule. By allowing an apparent schedule crisis to delete the performance of inspections, the manager actually will be *minimizing* the product quality, *maximizing* the cost, and adversely impacting the schedule which he thought was being assisted by the action of eliminating inspections. The inspection process, especially when coupled with the automated tools described in this book, will eradicate the need to rush into the test phase without adequate time being spent in the earlier phases. The level of product quality achieved as a result of performing all the inspections will be such that a minimum of 70 percent of the life cycle defects will already have been identified and removed during inspections—*before testing ever begins.*

The portion of the PDS for that software which has completed that I_1 inspection will be complete by the end of that inspection.

I_1 Data Analysis

Examples, from the same program as just referenced, of the type of I_1 inspection data available include, but are not limited to, the following:

1. Defect percentages: The major defects detected, and removed, during the I_1 inspections are shown by defect type,

as a percentage of the total major defects detected. This is the pie chart shown as Figure 4.5.

2. Defect totals: The total major defects detected, by defect type. This data corresponds to the percentage data shown in Figure 4.5. This is the bar chart shown as Figure 4.6.

3. Defect density: The total defects, major and minor, detected and removed, per thousand source lines of code (KSLOC), during the I_1 inspections. This is the line chart shown as Figure 4.7.

4. Inspection efficiency: The I_1 inspection process effectiveness is shown in summary form by the data in Figures 4.5, 4.6 and 4.7. The efficiency is measured in terms of the number of manhours expended to conduct the inspection process (not including the time to fix the defects found) per major defect detected. This is shown in Figure 4.8.

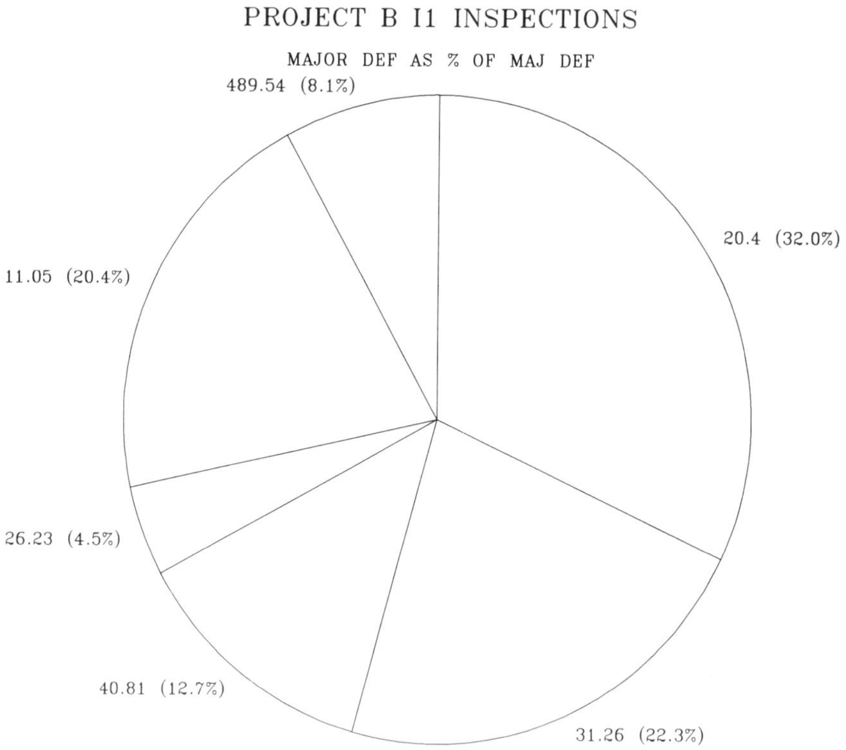

PROJECT B I1 INSPECTIONS

MAJOR DEF AS % OF MAJ DEF

489.54 (8.1%)

20.4 (32.0%)

11.05 (20.4%)

26.23 (4.5%)

40.81 (12.7%)

31.26 (22.3%)

Figure 4.5 Project B I_1 Inspections Pie Chart Showing Defect Type as Percentage of Total Major Defects Detected

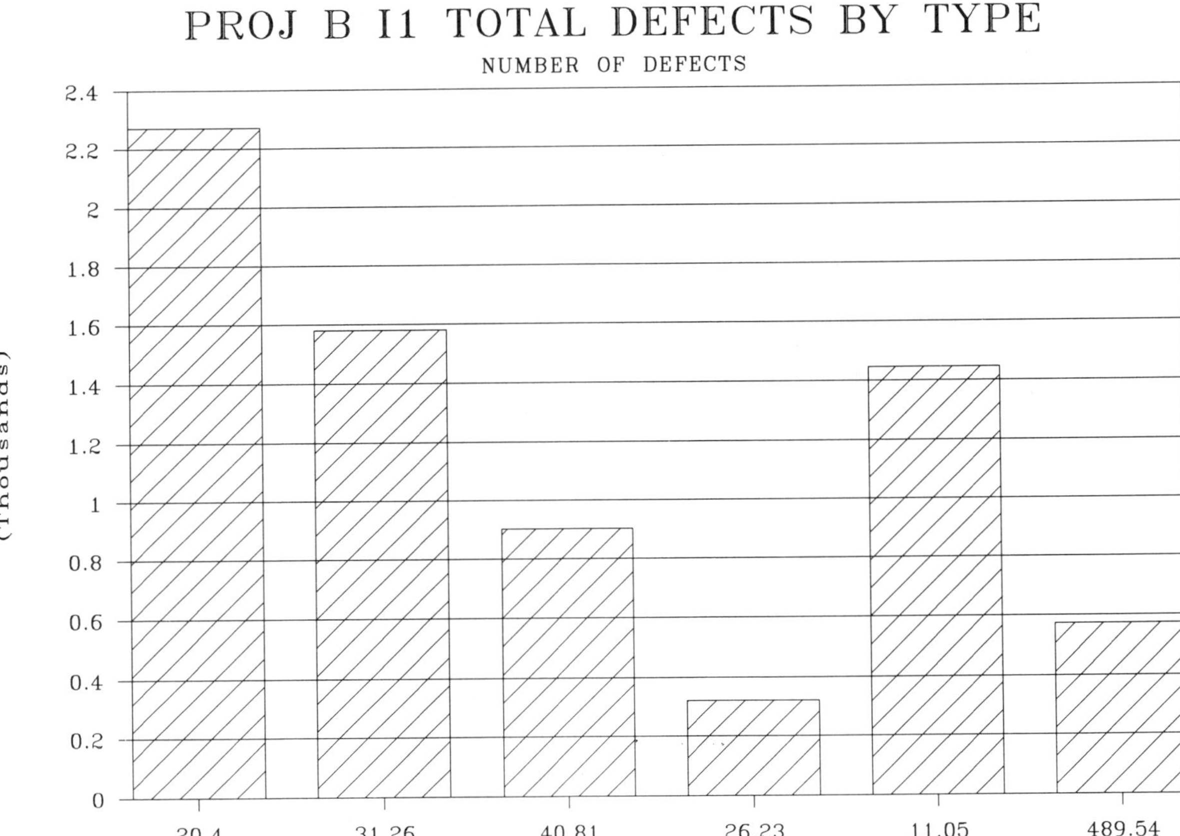

Figure 4.6 Bar Chart of Project B I_1 Total Defects by Type

Figure 4.7 Line Chart Displaying Density of Project B I_1 Inspections

Figure 4.8 Project B I_1 Inspection Measurement of Inspection Process Efficiency

5. Individual defect data: Other charts showing data related to individual defect types, such as the density of design defects over a period of time, are available, but not included here in the interest of saving space.

Code Inspections (I_2)

A code inspection (I_2) is held for all new code, code from another task which is being modified to meet the requirements of the new task or contract, or code modified as a result of a program trouble report (PTR) fix being implemented. The code inspection is not performed until after there has been an error-free compile. All six phases of the inspection process (with the possible exception of the overview phase) are conducted for each I_2. In some cases where there is a very minor program trouble report (PTR) fix, the lead programmer may decide not to hold an I_2 inspection. There should be a person designated with the responsibility to make this judgment. This decision is purely technical and not one driven by schedule.

Purpose of the Code Inspection (I_2)

The code inspection, in addition to finding defects, will serve the following purposes before proceeding with program test functions.

1. Verification that the code conforms to the PPS, PDS, and IDS requirements for operational software.

2. Confirmation that the design has been correctly converted to the target language.

3. Verification that the code conforms to the on-line diagnostic software requirements where there may be on-line interface.

4. Early audit of code quality by the programmer's peers.

5. Early detection of errors.

6. Verification that the code meets level-to-level module interface requirements.

7. Review of module unit test specification, which is provided with the inspection materials package.

8. Verification that the module test specifications (module test plan) are necessary and sufficient to test the requirements specified for that module and reviewed during the design inspections (I_0 and I_1).

9. Verification that the proper test tools and test environment have been identified and are available.

10. Verification that the test dependencies are correct and the module is testable based on the dependencies.

11. Verification that the module is ready to begin unit test.

12. Verification that the software products conform to the contract or internal standards and conventions.

Code inspections for each software module are typical of the type of pass/fail events which will serve as key entry/exit management milestones in the software development schedule.

The result of the successful completion of code inspection should be a completely coded module which conforms to the high-level design, low-level design and the PPS.

Only after successful completion of the code inspection can the module unit test begin.

I_2 Data Analysis

Examples, from the same program as referenced previously, of the I_2 inspections include, but are not limited to, the following:

1. Defect percentages: The major defects detected and removed during the I_2 inspections are shown by defect type, as a percentage of the total major defects detected. This is the pie chart shown as Figure 4.9.

2. Defect totals: The total major defects detected, by defect type. This data corresponds to the percentage data shown in Figure 4.9. This is the bar chart shown as Figure 4.10.

3. Comparative defect density: The total defects, major and minor, detected and removed, per thousand source lines of code (KSLOC), during the I_0, I_1, and I_2 inspections. This is the bar chart shown as Figure 4.11. The level of consistency in both application of the inspection process and measurement of the inspection data, produces the consis-

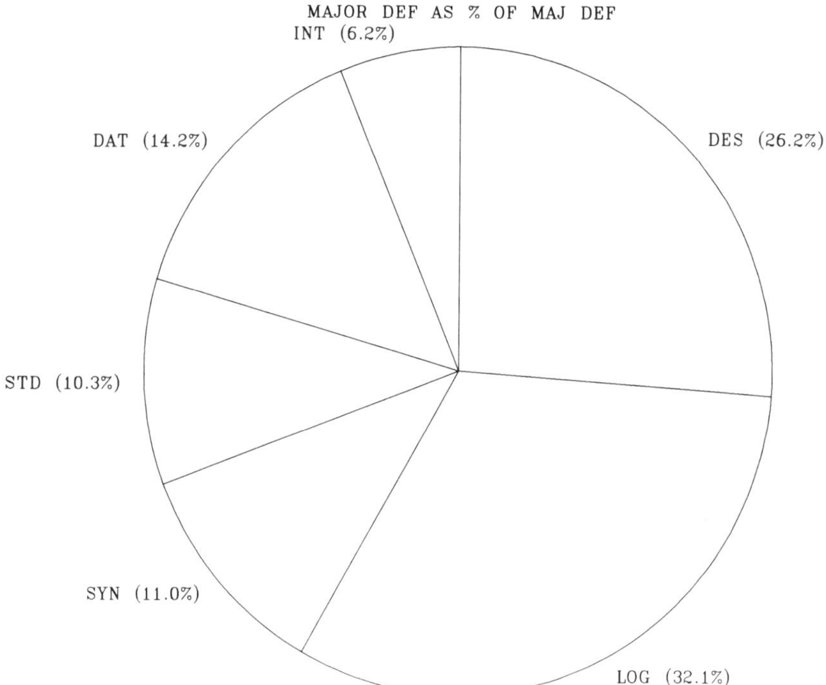

Figure 4.9 Project B I_2 Inspections Pie Chart Showing Defect Type as Percentage of Total Major Defects Detected

tency in results allowing for the establishment of the entry/exit criteria necessary for quality management at these early phases of the life cycle.

4. Comparative inspection efficiency: The comparative inspection process effectiveness is shown in summary form by the data in Figure 4.11. The efficiency is measured in terms of the number of manhours expended to conduct the inspection process (not including the time to fix the defects found) per major defect detected. This comparative data is shown in Figure 4.12.

5. Cost analysis: When the inspection process is applied to a project, the primary objective of early detection and removal of defects, is both technically desirable and cost-effective. The cost of a defect's removal at these early phases is approximately one-tenth, or less, the cost of removing a defect during integration or system test. During the test phases, the manpower expenditures, the computer

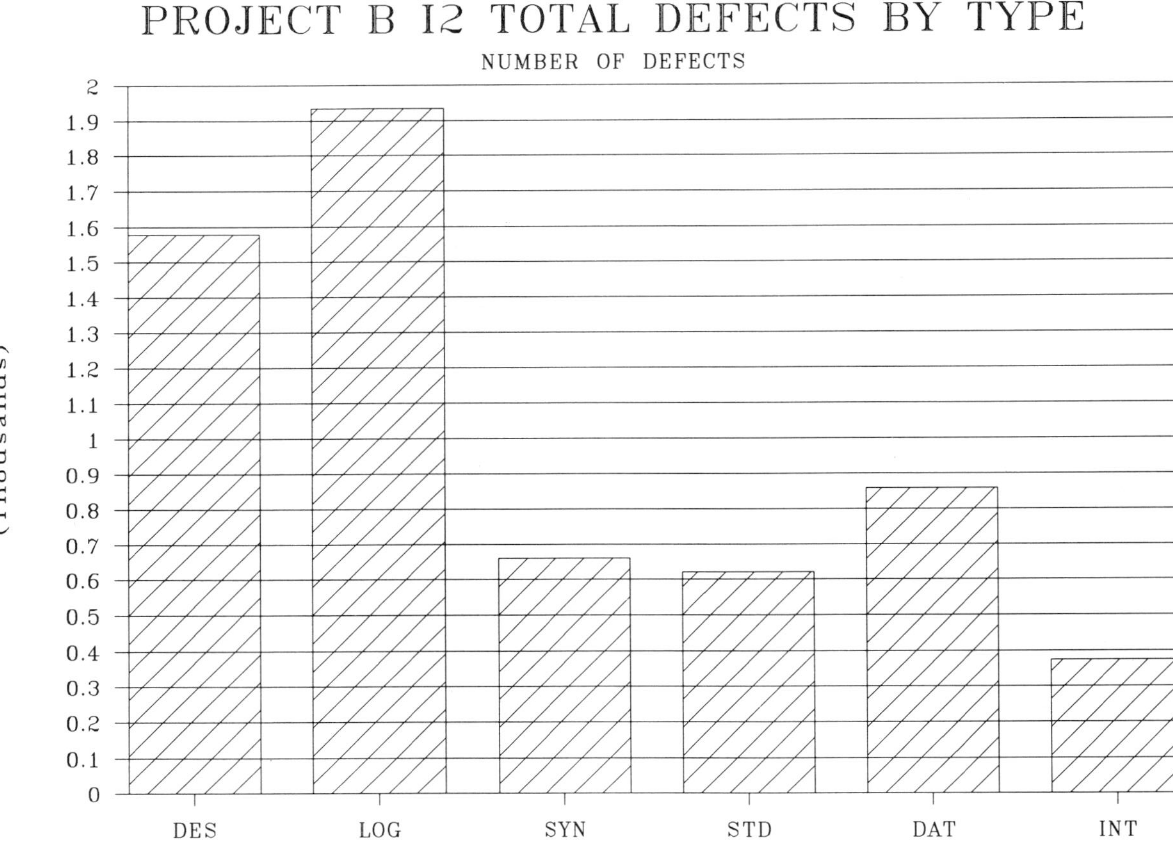

Figure 4.10 Bar Chart of Project B I_2 Total Defects by Type

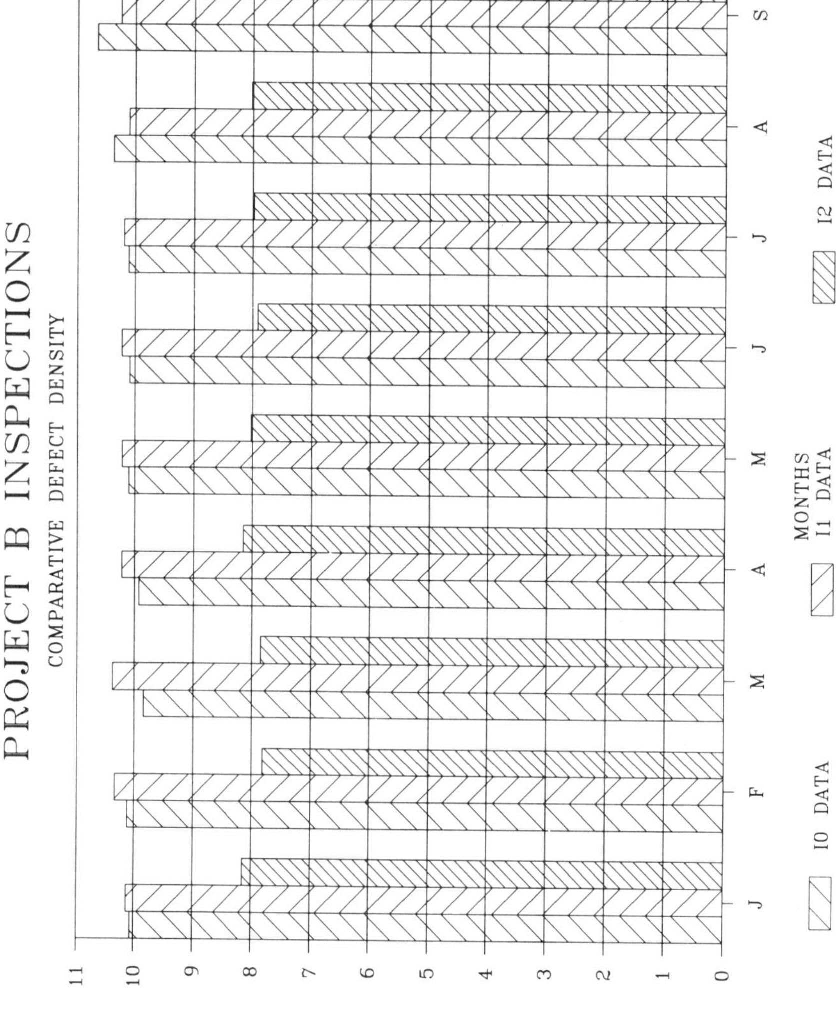

Figure 4.11 Bar Chart of Project B Showing Total Defects Detected and Removed per Thousand Lines of Code, during I_0, I_1, and I_2 Inspections

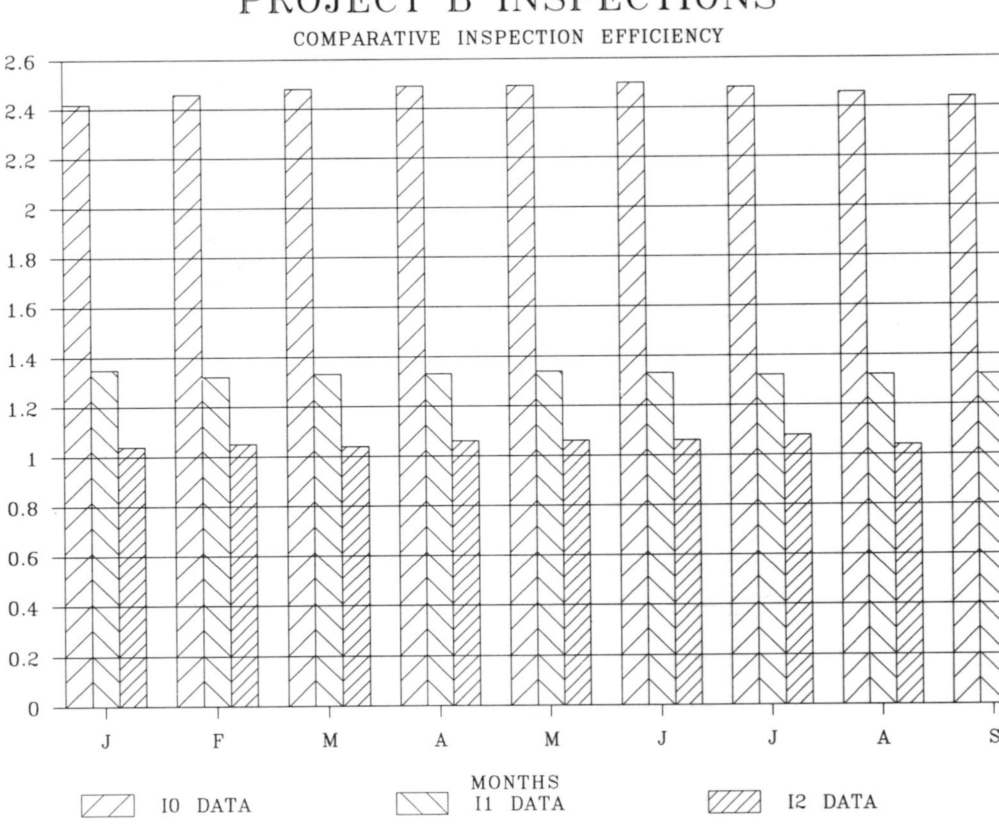

Figure 4.12 Project B Comparative Data of Efficiency in Manhours Expended to Conduct Inspection Process per Major Defects Detected

and other equipment resources required, and the time required, all contribute to the cost and inefficiency of defect correction. To gain insight, and therefore *management,* of the cost factors related to software defect detection and removal, the real cost benefits of the inspection process must be known. This is provided in Figures 4.13 and 4.14. The cost avoided (not incurred) as a result of doing inspections is:

a. The cost which would have been required to fix the major defects detected during inspections if they were not found until the integration and system test phases, otherwise referred to herein as raw cost (an average cost of $2,000 per defect was chosen for these charts, even though the costs reported in general literature are $7,000 and up), minus

b. The total manpower cost of exercising the inspection process (for the sake of this example, an average figure of $40 per manhour was chosen), plus the cost of fixing all of the defects (major and minor) found during the inspections (an average cost of $150 per defect was chosen).

These costs are provided in two charts, showing:

1. The raw cost avoided, compared to the total lines of code produced (Figure 4.13), and

2. The net cost avoided (**a** minus **b,** above) compared to the cost of performing the inspections. This shows the real cost avoided as well as the investment required (inspection cost) to achieve these net results (Figure 4.14).

Inspection Initiation

Inspections are initiated upon the completion of software design, either high- or low-level, or upon the completion of the first clean compile of code following initial development or maintenance modification. Developers will not spend any time doing desk-checking of the product once these conditions have been met.

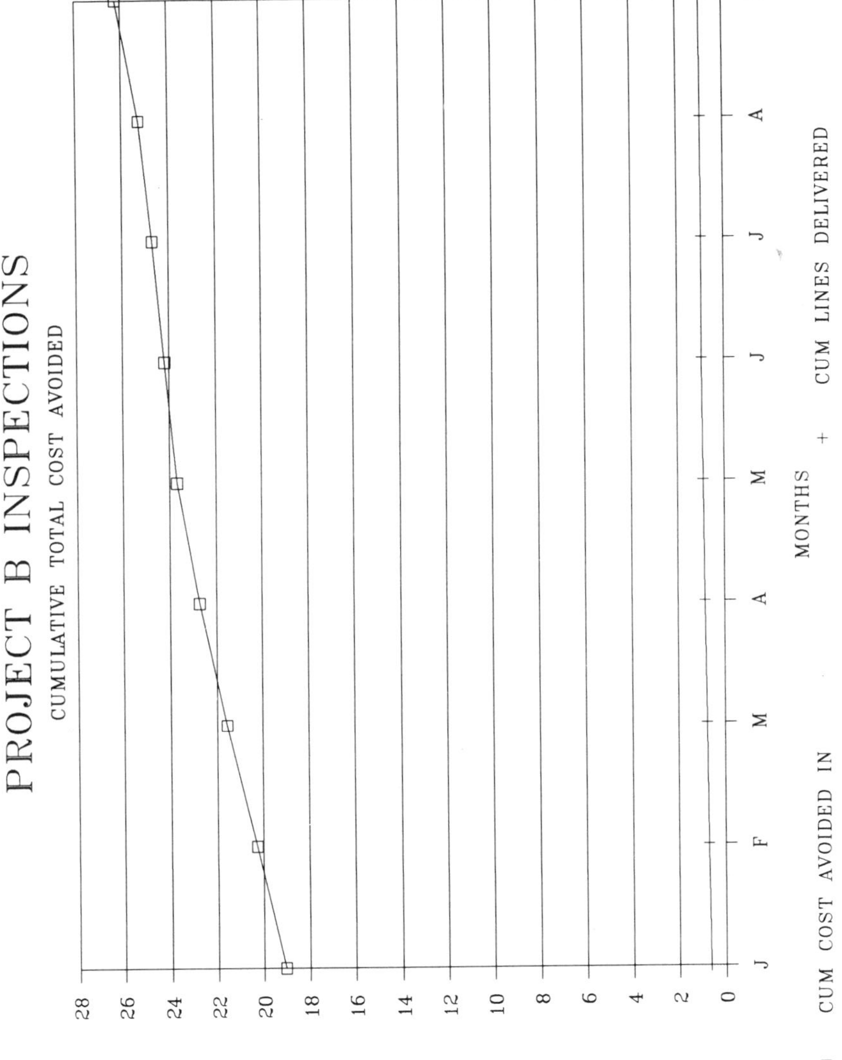

Figure 4.14 Project B Inspections Chart of Costs Avoided and Incurred

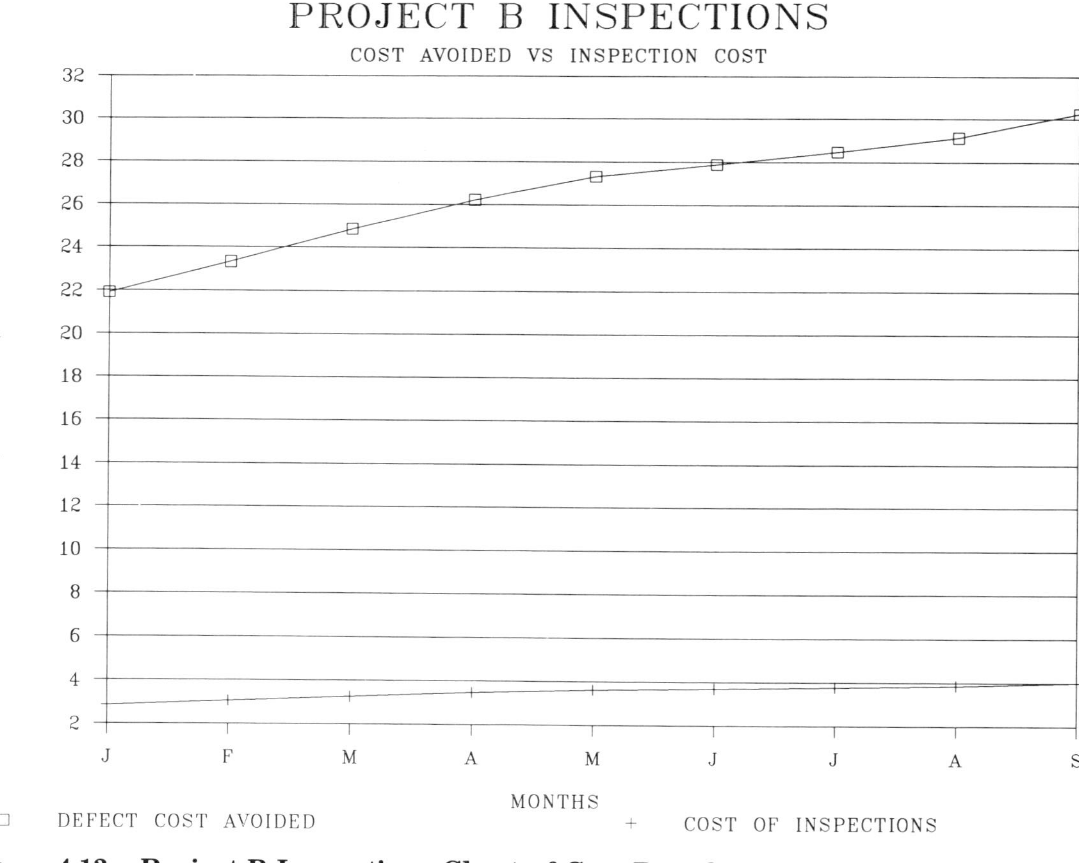

Figure 4.13 Project B Inspections Chart of Cost Benefits

Inspection Prerequisites

The requirements for the proper conduct of an inspection meeting are:

1. A team of technically competent, trained inspectors.
2. A trained moderator.
3. Proper planning and distribution of materials.
4. A good, professional attitude.
5. Full preparation *prior* to the inspection meeting.
6. Completed design or cleanly compiled code.
7. Updated resource requirements.

Data Collection

The maximum benefit from the inspection process is achieved when the process is applied *consistently*. To achieve this consistency, SQA should design and utilize a set of data collection forms for utilization throughout the inspection process on all tasks where this process is implemented. These forms are designed for the inspectors to use during the preparation period and for the moderator to use when producing the inspection's summary. These forms also serve as the input data mechanism for the inspection process data base.

Data Reporting

The summary data reports are provided to SQA and the information is entered into the SQA inspection data base. From this data base, SQA will publish the set of statistical charts showing graphically, and in some cases digitally, the summary cumulative results and trends of all the inspections for a given project, and, if requested, the results for a given department or function. Examples of some of the charts which can be produced have been provided in Figures 4.1 through 4.14.

Productivity Benefits of the Inspection Process

Productivity is not achieved when the work done has to be redone because of *avoidable* errors. Every line of code which is changed because of an avoidable error constitutes a loss of a line of productivity. Although customers often live in an environment where schedule priorities are a reality, the end product produced for the customer must still perform its function. Otherwise, all the schedule induced shortcuts conceivably implemented are merely wasted effort. This continually places the customer in a position where lack of early visibility leads to both technical and financial crisis situations forcing the customer to accept a product known to be defective. The post-delivery maintenance costs become prohibitive and the overall mission of the system into which the product must function is impaired.

The cost-effective results of the inspection process, and the management visibility and control afforded by the inspection process, will be lost if an apparent schedule crisis is the rationale for entering or exiting a low-level design or code phase too early. The errors found later in test (or even after delivery), instead of during the inspections will require more time to fix, will be more difficult to fix, will require more manpower resources to test and implement the fix, will require greater computer resources, and will be considerably more costly to implement. The fixes entered in such an environment are more error-prone, introduce greater module complexity, impact the module maintainability, and in most cases ultimately work adversely to the intent and mission of the product and user.

Use of Automated Tools During Inspection

The inspection process as described previously is a fundamentally manual process. The cost data shown in Figures 4.13 and 4.14 are based on the inspection process having been manually implemented. However, it should be clear from what was seen in Chapter 3 that the combination of the inspection process with automated source code analyzers, such as the Logiscope automated tool, will result in a much less time-consuming process, greater cost benefits, and much lower inspection costs. The principal activities of the inspections, especially if the software design is written in PDL or Ada (design languages for which there are Logiscope analyzers available), will principally focus on the software's function, thereby allowing Logiscope to provide the analysis data for detection of the remainder of the defects usually detected.

In addition, since the unit test requirements and plans are often examined as a part of the code inspection, some additional options of Logiscope are quite useful. The test aid option provides the programmer with an analysis of the module which identifies the decision-to-decision paths (DDP), identifies the source code line number for each construct, identifies the type of decision, and identifies the decision conditions (see Chart 4.1).

DDP	Line Number	Type	Condition
1	1	Begin	
2	263	Do-Loop	I = 1, 15
3	265	End-Do-Loop	
4	272	Structured-If	CONFIG >= 2 and CONFIG < 9
5	277	Structured-If	ANSWER = 'n' or ANSWER = 'N'
6	278	Do-Loop	I = 4, 8
7	280	End-Do-Loop	
8	281	Do-Loop	I = 10, 14
9	283	End-Do-Loop	
10	284	Else	not (ANSWER = 'n' or ANSWER = 'N')
11	285	Else	not (CONFIG >= 2 and CONFIG < 9)
12	294	Structured-If	IN_COLOR
13	296	Do-Loop	I = 0, 15
14	298	End-Do-Loop	
15	299	Else	not (IN_COLOR)

List of DDP for module
BZONE_SCREEN_INIT

Chart 4.1 Logiscope's Test Aid Option Identifies Decision-to-Decision (DDP) Paths

This test aid allows the programmer to develop test cases which will assure 100 percent coverage of the module paths. It will not assure total coverage for all *possible* paths, but will provide the information required to build the test cases covering all independent paths. When completed, the programmer is assured that every path of the module is exercised at least once, and the number of times each has been exercised is known exactly.

When the test cases are run, the dynamic analysis provisions of Logiscope provide an analysis of the test coverage, by DDP, showing the DDP numbers, the number of times each was exercised by each test, the percent of the module covered by the test, and the total percentage of the module covered by all of the tests combined (Chart 4.2). It also provides a graphic picture of the results, in the form of a control graph, showing the paths covered as solid lines and the paths not covered as dashed lines (Figures 4.15, 4.16 and 4.17).

When all of the modules are considered, Logiscope provides a histogram showing, as a function of the percent of the modules tested, the percent coverage of the modules as a result of the tests identified, given in coverage groups of 10 percent. Clearly, the ideal situation is where 100 percent of the modules are covered 100 percent by the tests run. (Figure 4.18).

Summary

The advantages of the inspection process can be summarized as follows:

- Extensive management visibility and control is provided.
- A large percentage of life-cycle defects are removed before test ever begins.
- Test time, and normal SQA test monitoring requirements are reduced.
- Programmers spend minimal time in software debug tasks.
- Development schedules are more easily controlled and managed.
- Significant development costs can be avoided, thereby preventing large contract overruns.
- Rework is minimized.

When used in combination with automated analysis tools, the benefits of inspections in and of themselves are multiplied considerably.

Note

1. Fagan, M. E., "Design and Code Inspections to Reduce Errors in a Program Development." *IBM Systems Journal,* No. 3 (July 1976), pp. 182–207.

DDP / Tests	1	2	3	4	5	6
TEST1	641	0	641	0	641	1
TEST2	376	0	376	0	376	1
TEST3	91	0	91	0	91	2
Total	1108	0	1108	0	1108	4

DDP / Tests	7	8	9	10	11	12
TEST1	640	5	2	3	3	0
TEST2	375	4	1	3	3	0
TEST3	89	3	0	3	3	0
Total	1104	12	3	9	9	0

DDP / Tests	13	14	15	16	17	Rate of Coverage
TEST1	636	0	641	1	640	76%
TEST2	372	2	374	2	372	82%
TEST3	88	1	90	1	89	76%
Total	1096	3	1105	4	1101	82%

DDP coverage rate of module
BZONE_UPDATE_DISPLAY

Chart 4.2 Logiscope's Dynamic Analysis Provisions Show Analysis of Test Coverage by DDP

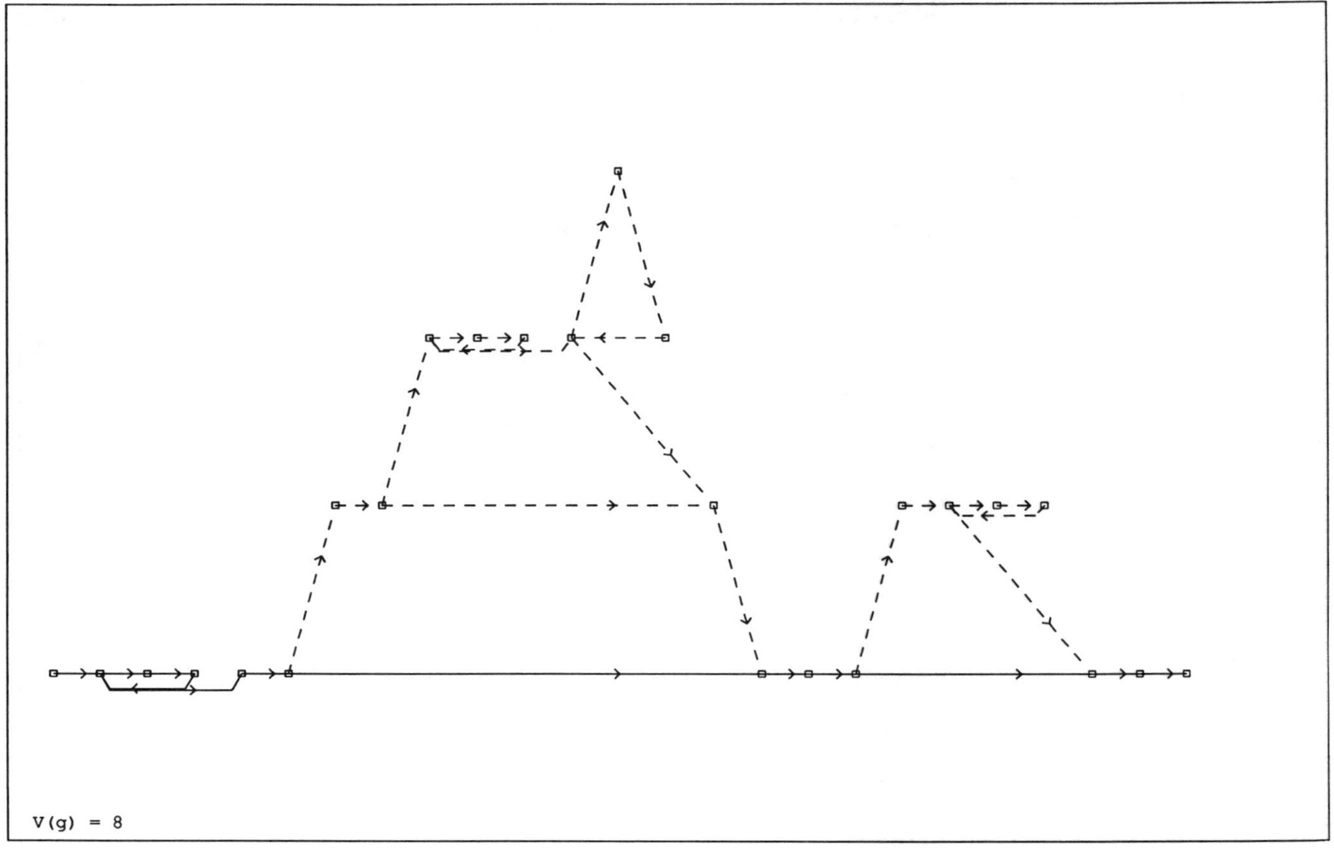

Figure 4.15 Graphic Picture of Test Results Provided by Logiscope

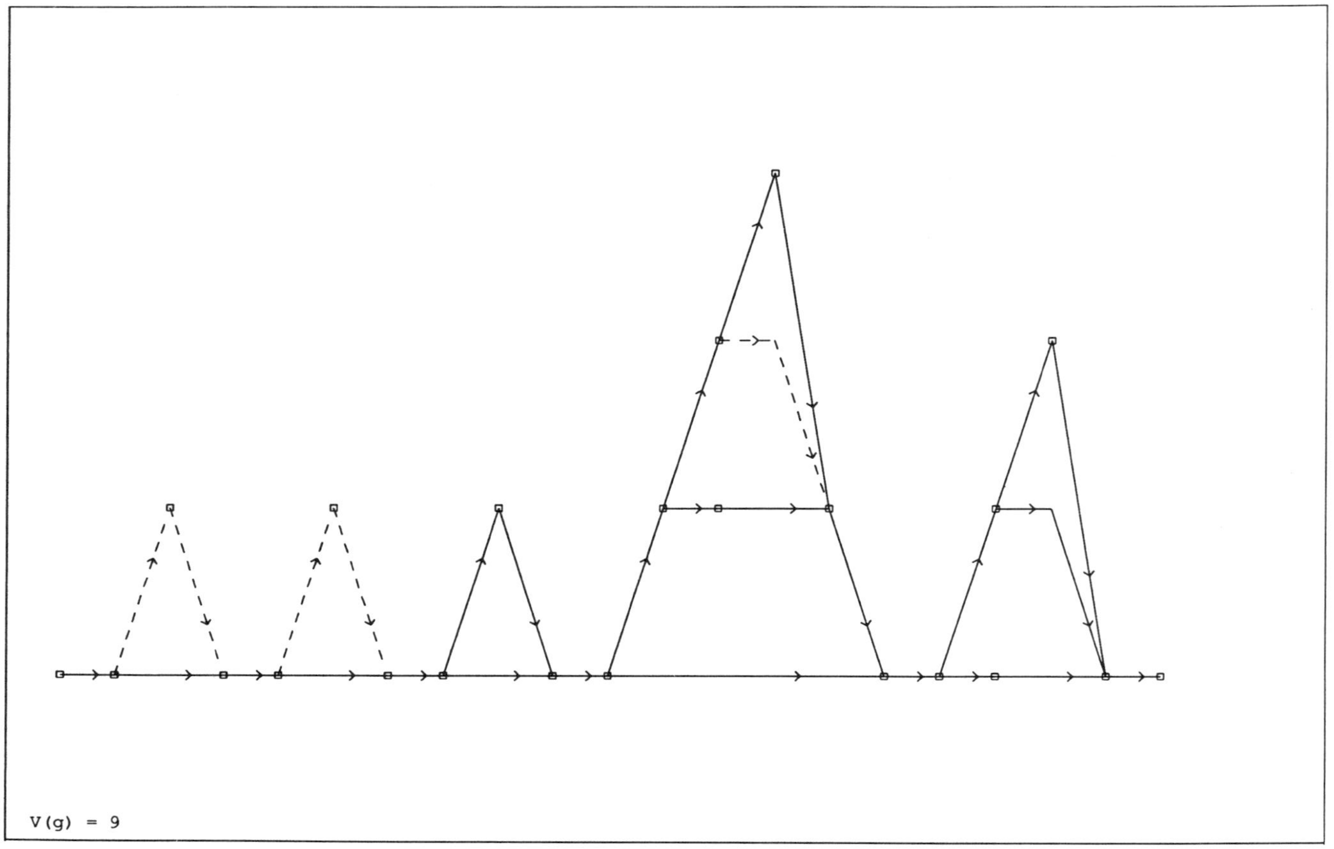

Figure 4.16 Graphic Picture of Test Results Provided by Logiscope

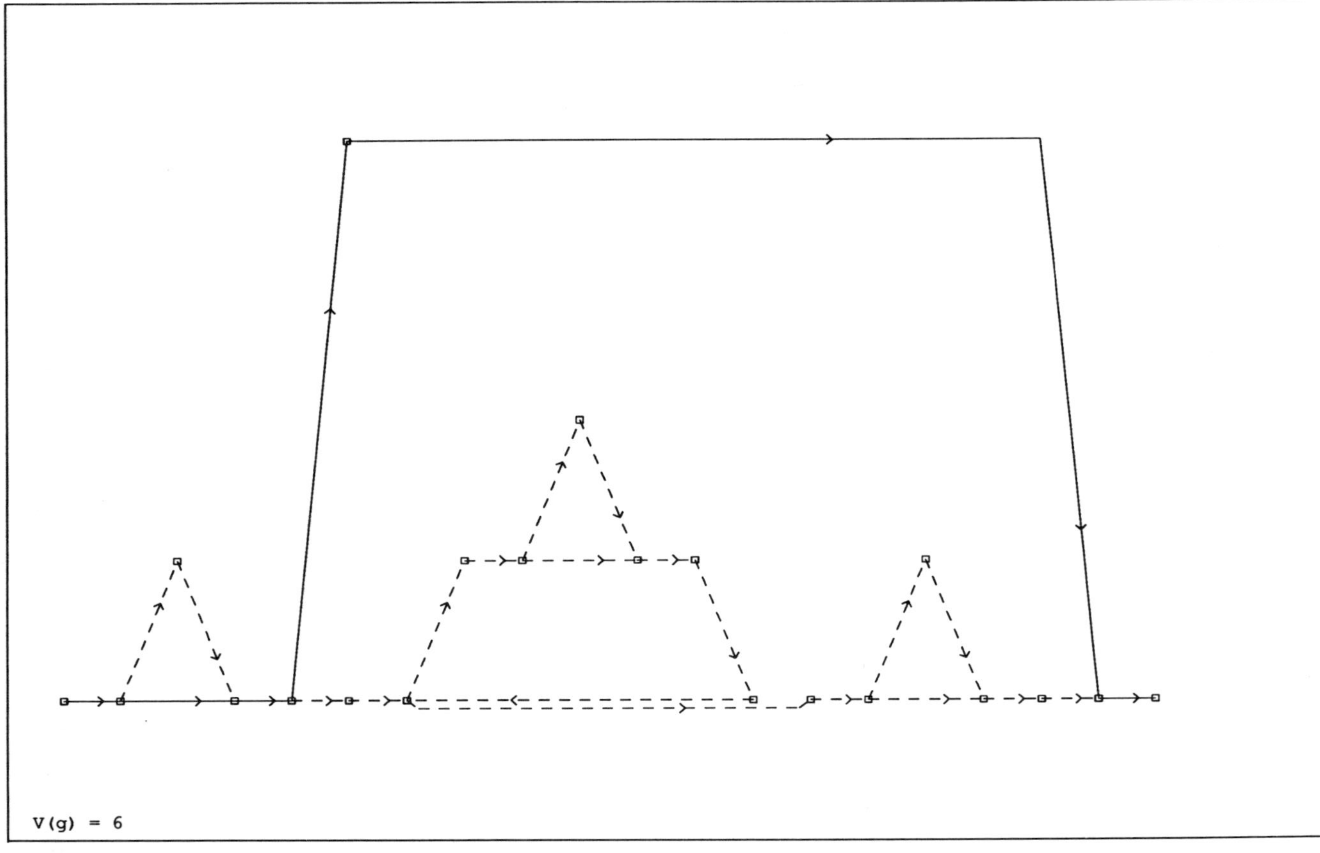

Figure 4.17 Graphic Picture of Test Results Provided by Logiscope

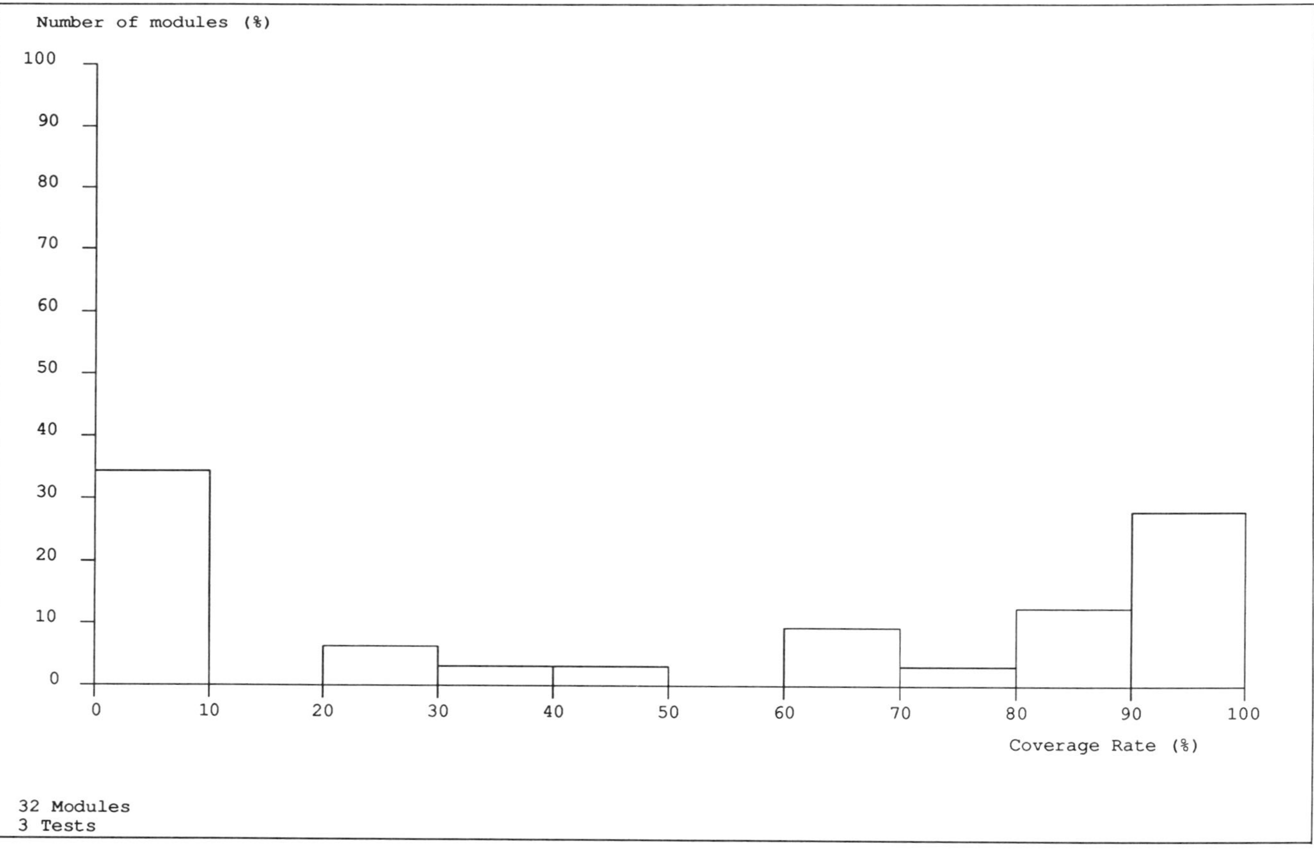

Figure 4.18 Logiscope Histogram Displaying Percent Coverage of Modules as Result of Identified Tests

CHAPTER 5

DOCUMENT INSPECTIONS

SQA has the responsibility for software document inspection. This involves the inspection of the documents for compliance with the standards imposed on a contract, or compliance with internal company standards.

Where contractual standards are imposed, the standards usually define the format and content required for the documents being delivered. This examination process can be done manually, in which case the document is read and the results are noted on a document review form developed for that purpose. As a minimum, the document title, revision number, control number, project or contract name, reviewer name, review date, accept/reject indication, and a summary of any discrepancies noted should be included.

This completed document inspection form is retained by SQA as a part of the SQA objective evidence. The SQA procedures manual should define the document inspection process and contain a copy of the document inspection form. A copy of the completed form should be sent to the document originator and the original retained as objective evidence. An example of a simple document inspection form is included in Appendix F.

If the document is rejected, the reasons should be very clearly noted along with a statement of what is required to remove the rejection.

If possible, SQA should certify the use of document creation tools. The use of automated tools which assist in the development of software documents which conform to the requirements for format and structure, as specified in the applicable standard and data item description (DID), are a considerable time-saver.

Care should be taken, of course, to always be assured that the automated tool matches the particular revision level of the standard or DID describing the required content of the deliverable item.

In addition, with the advent of DoD-STD-2167A and DoD-STD-2168, the possibility of the document requirements having to be modified as a result of the tailoring of the standards must be considered.

Customer Approval

Some documents that are developed under contract require customer approval. In such instances, the document should never be delivered without having been reviewed and approved by SQA. Any instance of disapproval by SQA should mean that the document does not conform to contract requirements, and it makes no sense to deliver a document to the customer which is known to be out of conformance with the contract requirements.

There are two ways that a document can be delivered to the customer under a government contract. The documents can be delivered via letter of transmittal (LT), which is the most common means, or by DD250. A DD250 document means that the Defense Contract Administration Services (DCAS), or other such government agency, personnel must review and accept the document. An LT delivery means that the document is sent to the customer under a cover letter, and the customer has a certain number of days within which to comment or the document is considered as accepted by the customer. If accepted, the contractor is entitled to payment for that item. The number of days within which comments must be received by the contractor is usually specified in the contract.

Acceptance Test Procedures

Acceptance test procedures is one type of document usually delivered to the customer for approval. The approval must be received before the test is run.

However, assuming that this approval process has taken place, it still is necessary to gain further customer approval for any changes. During the conduct of the acceptance test, or the dry run which should precede such a test, there may be some steps of the procedure which require change of one sort or another. In such an instance, a properly authorized customer representative must sign off on each change, usually classified as a "red-line" change. The final acceptance test is run using the official red-lined procedure containing the customer approval indications, some of the changes possibly being made during the acceptance test.

Following completion of the acceptance test, this red-lined copy of the acceptance test procedure should be retained by SQA under bonded storage. It is the only record available showing specific customer-approved changes, and which specifies the customer representative responsible for the approval. Sometimes, software CM or engineering records, in order to meet readability requirements, will attempt to republish the redlined copy with the changes incorporated. In that way, so it is argued, a "clean" copy is available for reproduction. Even if a management decision is made to republish, the original redlined copy should always be retained under bonded control by SQA.

CHAPTER 6

SOFTWARE CONFIGURATION CONTROL

Software configuration control is fundamentally the process whereby the software integrity is maintained and the progression from one version of the software to the next is achieved in an orderly and certifiable manner. There are several elements all forming the basis for an effective configuration control process.

SQA Bonded Storage

The SQA bonded storage facility is the repository where the master copies of the software under development, or the master copies of government- or subcontractor-delivered software, are kept. The proper administration of the storage facility is dependent upon the record keeping procedures. Fundamental to the proper development of the configuration control storage facility is the creation of an accurate and easily manipulated data base. The data base should be able to track the status of every item included in or controlled by the storage facility administrator.

The data base should, for each item included, identify the project name; the type of media (tape, diskette, listing, etc.); the date when the item entered the storage facility; whether the item is the master or a copy and, if a copy, the identification of the master; the media ID (such as tape or diskette number); the ID of the software itself (such as the part number if such an identification system is employed, or the software name and version number, or other appropriate identification); the location of the media (in the storage area or signed out to another department); and whether the item is an in-process development version, a final delivered version, or a customer- or subcontractor-delivered product.

The ID of the software must be unique and the ID system must be describable and included in the SQA procedures manual. If a part number system is employed, the part number of the software will have an identifying and accompanying drawing which describes, in detail, the unique components of the software, including the list of component modules and their version numbers.

Each change in condition of the data base items should be recorded immediately. At any time, SQA should be able to identify every item in the storage area, and the status and location of each item. The storage area, and the data base, are subject to customer audit. If the customer is a government agency, the SQA storage facility is particularly important because the software which is acceptance-tested is the copy provided by SQA to the test conductor at the time of the test. If the government auditors have no confidence in the integrity of the SQA facility, then the acceptance test result itself is questionable. It also presents problems with the requirement for SQA to certify the contractor's compliance with the standards' requirements.

For a large development facility with several ongoing software projects, some being perhaps millions of lines of code, the maintenance of the storage facility and data base is a full-time job for more than just one person. A casual approach to this task will guarantee an SQA bonded storage facility which will never be able to serve its intended purpose, and will never pass a government audit.

Software Change Control Board (SCCB)

The SCCB is the board which governs the creation and modification of the controlled library system. The board is composed of representatives from various departments, including software development, software engineering, SQA, software control, configuration management, and software test.

At or before the time of the formation of the SCCB, the SCCB procedures should be written and a determination made of which members are mandatory and which are required to constitute a quorum. As a minimum, SQA and CM should be included in the quorum.

The procedures also should clearly address such issues as whether the build approval requires unanimous or only a majority vote of the SCCB members present. Although a majority vote is a normal instinctive choice, consideration should be given to a requirement for a unanimous vote. The pressures of schedule and cost may drive some members to cast votes for inclusion of software even though that software has been inadequately tested, or where the fix to a module has not yet been validated, or perhaps even where the software is known to be defective. This is especially true where the program manager, or the representative of that office, is the SCCB's chairman. The SCCB should never be a rubber stamp, and should never base a decision only on schedule or cost if it is known that the product quality is deficient. For this reason, software CM or SQA should chair the SCCB.

Care also should be taken to assure that for every software change implemented, the corresponding software documentation also is updated. In some cases, the SCCB procedures have been established requiring the software documentation update before the software change is included in the build.

The SCCB decides if the software which is a candidate for inclusion in the controlled library has met the entry criteria. Entry criteria for a new module usually include, as a minimum, successful completion of unit test.

In instances where there is an effective software quality program, which involves defect prevention and removal processes early in the development cycle, the success of these processes, and the recording of their application, serves as an additional entry criterion. For example, where the inspection process is employed, the successful completion of all required inspections will be an entry criterion. It will be necessary for the SQA representative on the SCCB to have available data indicating the inspection status of the modules which are candidates for inclusion in the controlled library. The SQA representative should always have access to the inspection data related to the project to which he or she is assigned, and should have a data base of information detailing the modules which have been through the inspections, the current version number of each module, and which modules have completed unit test.

As the software proceeds through the integration test and system test phases, the module interfaces are tested, problem reports are written, and fixes are made. The fixes must be incorporated into the controlled library and new versions of the software made available for testing.

In many instances, the fixes are made and the test which resulted in the failure is rerun to show that the failure does not occur again.

Sometimes, a standard regression test is run. The regression test is supposed to show whether the change has caused other problems. The regression test, by its nature, presumes no change in the test paths or module complexity. However, the change process may well result in additional test paths through the software, and an increase in module complexity. Under these conditions, there is the possibility of the test path coverage dropping below a level required for the regression tests to maintain their integrity.

These tests are not expected to provide 100 percent coverage of all independent test paths, or 100 percent of all module calls, but there should be some minimal level of coverage for the tests to have the requisite integrity. If the test results analyzed show that the percent coverage has dropped below a level considered acceptable, then additional tests are added to the set of regression tests and the integrity is maintained.

The SQA representative, if access to an automated test path coverage analyzer such as Logiscope is available, will be able to invoke features like the control graph to determine if additional paths through the software module have been created by the fix and determine the exact percentage of path coverage at both the module and hierarchical level. This will be evident by comparison of the archived version of the module control graph prior to the change to the graph for the module version being offered as a candidate for inclusion in the controlled library.

If additional paths have been created, and if the module is still well-structured, and if only proper constructs are used, SQA should require additional unit tests to validate that the additional paths within the module cause no problem and do not create a condition which violates the specification.

In addition, where the tests run from the controlled libraries are integration tests or system tests, the interfaces between modules are important elements of the test. The call graph provides information graphically showing the interface structure between the modules, the top-down hierarchy, and also any conditions of recursive code (Figures 6.1, 6.2, and 6.3).

In the case of interface testing, the Logiscope interface test aid is available to the independent test department personnel to assist in determining the inter-module test paths. The procedure to procedure paths (PPP) are given, the calling modules are identified, and the called modules for each are identified (Chart 6.1).

When the integration tests are run, the results showing the tests run, the PPP identifiers, how many times each PPP is invoked, and the total path coverage percentage for each test as well as the cumulative coverage of all integration tests identified are provided. This provides a cumulative automated test coverage measure at the integration test phase (Chart 6.2).

The call graph for the integration tests also is available and the call paths tested between modules are shown as solid lines, and the paths not tested are shown as broken lines. This is a graphical representation of the data provided in Chart 6.2. An example of this is given in Figure 6.3.

Where such information is available to the SCCB, a decision based on sound information can be made in determining whether to incorporate the changed modules into the controlled library. If this information is used in conjunction with an effective library control system, the result will be a well-controlled software library configuration.

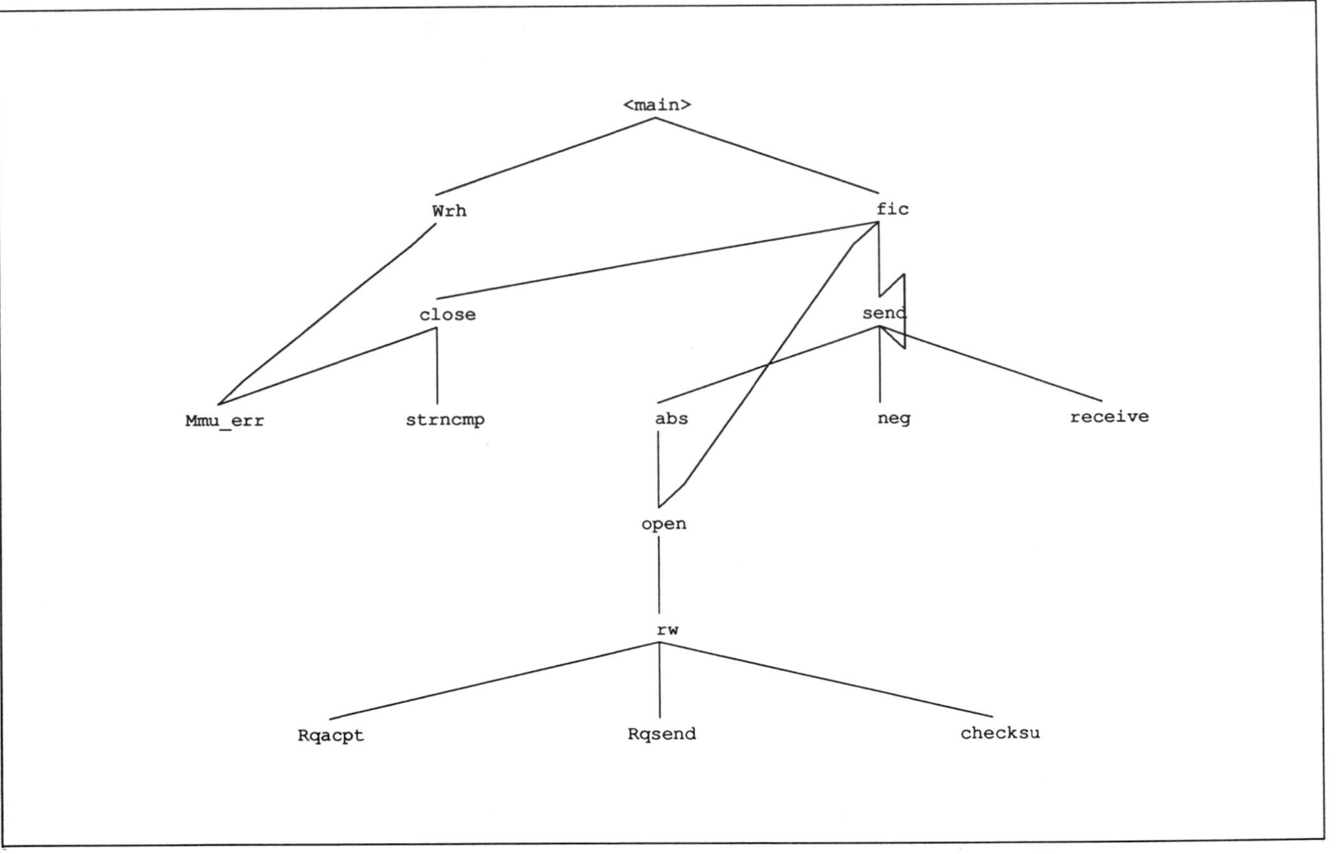

Figure 6.1 Call Graph of Main

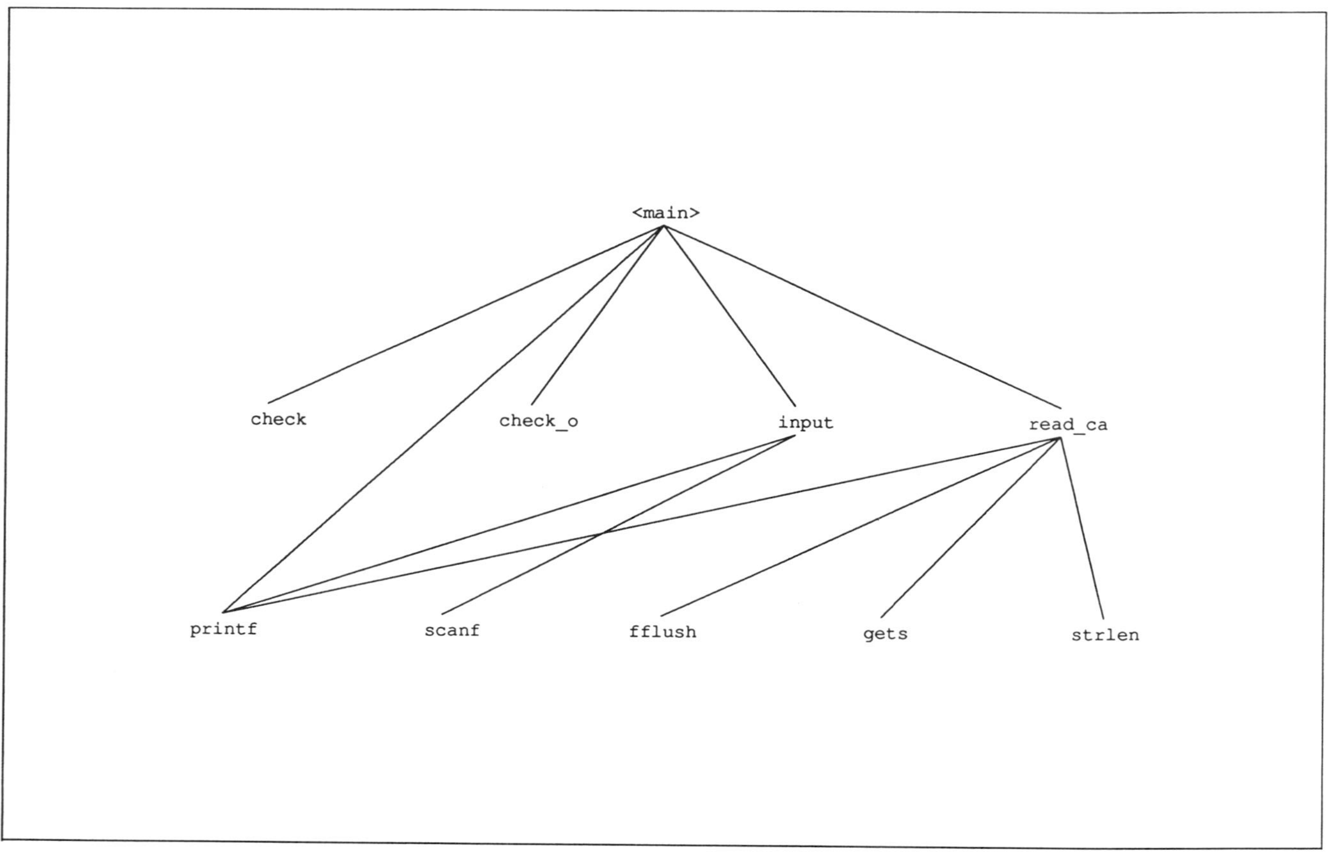

Figure 6.2 Call Graph for NEXTSYMBOL

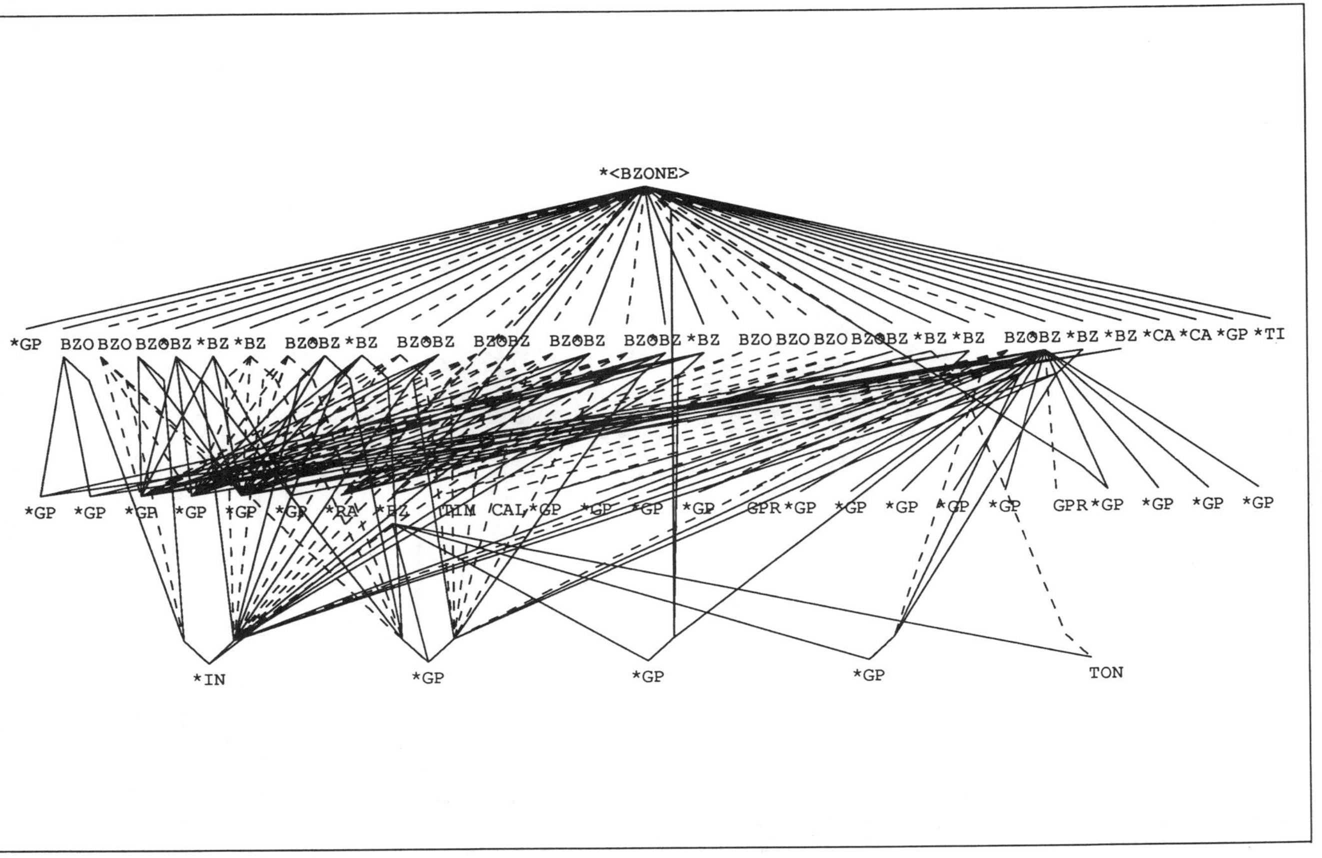

Figure 6.3 Call Graph of BZone Main

PPP	Calling Module	Called Module
1	BZONE_MAIN	GPR_$COND_EVENT_WAIT
2		BZONE_CLEAR_SCREEN
3		BZONE_DRAW_COPTER
4		BZONE_DRAW_CRACKS
5		BZONE_DRAW_CUBE
6		BZONE_DRAW_HORIZON
7		BZONE_DRAW_LANDER
8		BZONE_DRAW_MISSILE
9		BZONE_DRAW_PYRAMID
10		BZONE_DRAW_SALVO
150	BZONE_SCREEN_INIT	INT2
151		GPR_$CIRCLE
152		GPR_$CIRCLE_FILLED
153		GPR_$ENABLE_INPUT
154		GPR_$INIT
155		GPR_$INQ_CONFIG
156		GPR_$LOAD_FONT_FILE
157		GPR_$MOVE
158		GPR_$MULTILINE
159		GPR_$POLYLINE
160		GPR_$SET_CLIPPING_ACTIVE
161		GPR_$SET_CLIP_WINDOW
162		GPR_$SET_COLOR_MAP
163		GPR_$SET_CURSOR_POSITION
164		GPR_$SET_DRAW_VALUE
165		GPR_$SET_FILL_VALUE
166		GPR_$SE. .XT_BACKGROUND_VALUE
167		GPR_$SET_TEXT_FONT
168		GPR_$SET_TEXT_PATH
169		GPR_$SET_TEXT_VALUE
170		GPR_$TEXT
171		GPR_$TRAPEZOID
172	BZONE_UPDATE_DISPLAY	INT2
173		GPR_$BIT_BLT
174		GPR_$MOVE
175		GPR_$SET_RASTER_OP
176		GPR_$TEXT
177	BZONE_X_HAIRS	GPR_$MULTILINE
178		GPR_$SET_DRAW_VALUE

Chart 6.1 List of PPP for the Tree with BZone Main as Root

PPP / Tests	1	2	3	4	5	6
TEST1	3131	2	0	27	638	639
TEST2	1785	1	0	20	373	374
TEST3	401	0	0	0	87	89
Total	5317	3	0	47	1098	1102

PPP / Tests	7	8	9	10	11	12
TEST1	638	0	638	640	0	637
TEST2	373	0	373	375	0	373
TEST3	87	0	87	87	0	87
Total	1098	0	1098	1102	0	1097

PPP / Tests	169	170	171	172	173	174
TEST1	3	9	2	23	6	1
TEST2	3	9	2	23	8	1
TEST3	3	9	2	16	5	2
Total	9	27	6	62	19	4

PPP / Tests	175	176	177	178	Rate of Coverage
TEST1	4	1	328	328	56%
TEST2	2	1	193	193	53%
TEST3	0	2	47	47	52%
Total	6	4	568	568	60%

Chart 6.2 PPP Coverage Rate for the Tree with BZone Main as Root

SCCB Records

Minutes are kept for each SCCB identifying the members present, whether a quorum is present, the identification of software which is the candidate for inclusion in the controlled library (by module names and version numbers), whether or not the required inclusion criteria have been met, whether inclusion in the controlled library was authorized, the reasons for refusal if that is the decision, and the identification of those software documents which have been updated, or must be updated, to conform to the software change. The SCCB minutes are distributed to each SCCB member, and to the managers of each department represented on the SCCB.

The department which is responsible for accomplishing the software update (software control) is provided with a copy of the minutes, which serves as the authorization to incorporate the software in the controlled library.

Software Change Request

Part of the documentation provided to software control is the software change request (SCR). The SCR is that document which identifies the software to be incorporated, the location of the software (file ID and software ID), and any information required for software control to access the software and incorporate the changed module into the controlled library.

The SCR also identifies the reason for the change. This may be the initial entry of the module into the controlled library, or it may be the result of a software modification. If it is the result of a modification, the reason for the change is included, including the pertinent program trouble report (PTR) number(s).

The SCR is signed by SQA at the SCCB and this serves as the indication that the software being updated has met the quality criteria for inclusion in the controlled library. If the change is to government-provided software, or a delivered product, then a government representative also will be required to sign the change authorization. In some instances the government will waive this requirement, but it is still a government choice to do so, not a contractor prerogative.

CHAPTER 7
SQA TEST ACTIVITY

For many years the SQA activity was principally centered around the software test activity. Even today people talk about SQA testing. However, with the advances in software technology and software evaluation which have been made over the past few years, the idea of SQA testing is becoming an anachronism.

Rather than being a major part of the SQA activity, involvement in the test phases is now largely a matter of data analysis. A customer should never authorize the expenditure of funds for having SQA personnel watch others perform software testing. A requirement that SQA itself perform the testing is a decision which should not be made lightly. If SQA is responsible for certifying that the software development process has met all the requirements, and a part of those requirements is software test, it will require SQA certifying the performance of their own task. It is usually better to have an independent test team within the company perform the testing. In some cases, an outside company will perform this test, but for many projects this would be too costly and time-consuming. Whether or not this is done usually is left to the customer to decide and the independent test is performed under a separate independent verification and validation (IV&V) contract between the customer and the company performing the test.

SQA Test Data Analysis

The principal SQA activity during the test phases should be the analysis of program trouble report (PTR) data. Under conditions where the SQA department has an active role from the initiation of the project, the majority of the module defects should have been removed prior to the start of integration test. The software PTRs written should be primarily related to problems in the interface between the modules, or between the software and hardware.

Where inspections have been employed, the SQA PTR analysis should include an evaluation of the module level PTRs written, and a cross-check against the results of the inspections for that module. If the module was inspected successfully, SQA should determine when the lines of code which were incorrect were introduced. If they were part of the original module, the type of defect should be identified and a determination made of whether this defect type should have been found during the inspection. If trend analysis shows that this defect type is repeatedly found during test, the early defect prevention and removal processes should be examined to determine if this type of defect can be prevented or removed prior to test.

If the error was introduced later, the time of introduction should be determined and a judgment made as to whether the module should have been re-inspected. This information should be incorporated with similar information from other PTRs and an evaluation made of the need for modifying the inspection process itself. If other defect prevention and removal processes were employed, the same sort of analysis should be performed.

PTR Trend Analysis: Rate Charts

The rate of creation of the PTRs should be tracked by SQA and rate charts developed. If the time period from the beginning of the integration test period to the time of acceptance test is considered, the rate chart should have a predictable shape.

The time period between the end points of the test period should be identified, and the midpoint of the test period marked. If the project has had a reasonably effective initial defect prevention and removal process, the rate of PTR creation should begin to level off at about the midpoint of the test period (inflection point), and the curve representing this rate should begin to approach zero as an asymptote. Figure 7.1 shows this sort of rate chart based on data from an actual software development project. The only defect detection process employed early in the life cycle was the inspection process, and no automated analysis tools, such as have been discussed above, were employed.

If the software development process is not such that early defect detection and removal processes are employed, and the test period is regarded as the primary defect removal period, the likelihood of such a smooth and correctly shaped curve is low. The more likely condition will be a curve which is irregular in shape and which continues to rise throughout the test period. A rate chart with such a shape indicates that the project is not controlled, is unmanageable, and the software condition is such that high quality should not be expected.

If the SQA program is active, and if there are effective early defect removal processes employed, the curve will be properly shaped. The important thing to remember is that it is the shape of the curve which is important; much more so than the actual

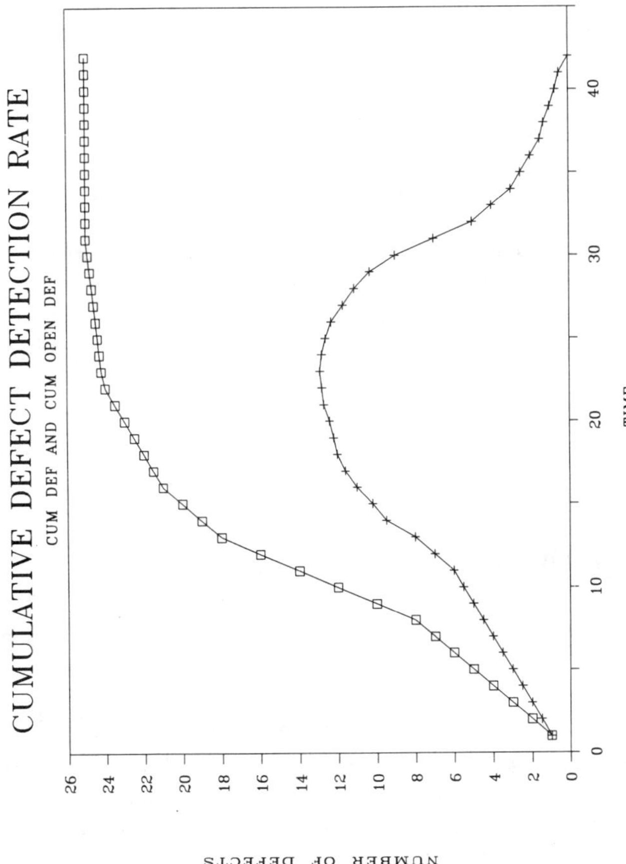

Figure 7.1 Rate Chart Displaying PTR Trend Analysis

count of the PTRs. If the shape of the curve is proper, the project is being well-managed and the risk of coming in over budget or behind schedule is minimized.

Where there is an effective program designed to improve the software development process, and improve the early defect prevention and removal processes, the effect can be seen by the impact it will have on the shape of the PTR rate chart. The general shape will remain basically the same, but the mid-test inflection point, that point where the curve begins to move sharply to the right and flatten out, will move gradually to the left. The further to the left this point of inflection moves, the more the software production process is improved.

As the inflection point moves to the left, the software increases in conformance with the requirements at the start of the test period. This gives the program manager an interesting option.

The software test period, instead of being the major period of defect detection and removal, becomes primarily a period of software validation. Once the software is validated, and depending on the nature of the software project and the intended use of the software, the program manager can either shorten the test phase, thereby reducing the schedule and cost, or use the allocated time to fine-tune the software in order to make it as robust as possible. There are advantages to either course of action.

SQA Test Monitoring

The dictates of the contract itself usually will require that specific types of tests be run. The contract standards may, and in the case of a government contract will, demand that SQA assure that all of the standards' requirements are accomplished. This means that, among other things, SQA will have to verify that the various required test phases are accomplished. This is usually done in part by the receipt of test data results, such as PTR data, and partly by in-person monitoring of the test activity. Having available the results of automated test coverage analyzers can significantly shorten the labor required for this task.

Test monitoring usually is accomplished by attendance at all, or a portion, of a sample of the tests run prior to acceptance test. The principal objective of the test monitoring is to verify that test procedures are being utilized, that the test environment is proper, that the software being tested is from the proper library, and to determine if there are any problems which might require more intensive SQA involvement. It is not an exhaustive test activity evaluation and analysis. The SQA representative maintains a log of the tests monitored and the results or conclusions of the monitoring. This is retained as a part of the objective evidence to be made available during customer audits.

SQA Test Witnessing

The difference between monitoring a test and witnessing a test is one of coverage. Test monitoring can be accomplished by sampling the tests monitored, and by attending all or only a part of the test monitored. Test witnessing is the attendance during, and evaluation of, a complete test or test series.

SQA should have initiated, or confirmed the application of, sufficient early defect prevention and removal processes so that the only test which will require test witnessing is the formal acceptance test. At this test, the SQA representative is a formal witness, along with the customer. The objective is:

- to assure that the customer-approved test procedure is followed;
- that any changes to the procedure are signed off by the customer and by SQA;
- to assure that the software tested is under SQA bonded control;
- that the pretest customer briefing includes the status of all known problems;
- that all output post-test media is secured by SQA and placed under control including the as-run test procedure;
- to obtain a copy of all PTRs written during the acceptance test; and
- to determine the extent to which the software conformed to the requirements as tested.

Following the acceptance test, a copy of the as-run procedure is given to the test conductor for use in writing the formal test report. A copy also is provided to configuration management so that an update to the machine version of the test procedure can be generated. This version will incorporate all the red-lines, but the customer sign-off or stamp cannot be transferred to the new version. Since there is only one master copy of the procedure, and only one record of the customer sign-off on any red-lines, this master copy is retained by SQA and entered into the SQA data library.

CHAPTER 8

SOFTWARE PROCUREMENT QUALITY ASSURANCE

SQA Procurement Quality Assurance Planning

For many projects, there will be certain elements for which a make-or-buy decision is made. A make-or-buy decision is a decision to develop the software in-house or contract for the development of that system or system component. In software, this can be the result of teaming agreements, or the decision that it is more cost-effective, or more technically feasible, for another company to develop certain functions. Sometimes this decision is a function of what hardware is being contributed by the subcontractor company. In a new system development, the company selected as a subcontractor often will provide both hardware and related software components of the system.

Contract Review

The first step in the process occurs during the RFP and subsequently during contract review processes conducted by SQA. The quality requirements are identified and related documents are created. These related documents are the SQA plan, the software quality evaluation plan, the applicability matrix, and audit (internal and subcontractor) checklists. Upon determination of the quality requirements, the set of requirements for any subcontractor also are determined. The prime contractor, and all software subcontractors, must adhere to the same requirements. Note that DoD-STD-2167 does not explicitly mandate this as did DoD-STD-1679A, but the requirement still is explicitly stated requiring SQA to certify that all requirements of the contract have been met. In most instances, this may be impossible unless the same quality requirements imposed on the prime contractor are also imposed on subcontractors.

Vendor Surveys

If a decision to subcontract has been made, but a contractor has not been selected, it will be necessary to perform vendor surveys. The surveys will be conducted prior to the bidders' conference, and will require funding from the program manager. The vendor surveys should not take any more than two days, and should be driven by a checklist so that a scoring of the vendor can be accomplished as objectively as possible.

In accomplishing the vendor survey, a checklist similar to the first checklist shown in Appendix E is helpful. It is very specific as to the document the vendor is being surveyed against, and the items of investigation are detailed and referenced to the specific paragraph numbers. At this level of detail, the ability to answer the questions to the maximum extent possible with a "Yes" or "No" will serve to help make the survey as objective as possible. Once a checklist of this type is created for the document in force on the contract, the SQA representative is able to score the results by indicating a score factor for each item or group of items. Each item (question) should be scored a certain number (possibly a 0 or 1) depending on the answer to the question, and then each item should be weighted in accordance with a criticality factor for that project or governing document. The weighted sum will be the score and will provide a relatively objective evaluation (at least as objective as possible given that the audit, being performed by humans, will necessarily be somewhat subjective). This degree of objectivity will be important if there are several potential subcontractors and the same SQA representative is not performing all of the vendor surveys.

Once the vendor survey is completed, the SQA representative should execute the scoring, and also write a survey report. This report should indicate the vendor score, the evaluation of the vendor in terms of the project mission, any areas which will require immediate correction, an assessment of the ability of the subcontractor to effect the correction(s) within the required time and without assistance from the prime contractor, an assessment of the apparent willingness of the vendor to make the required corrections (necessarily subjective judgments, and therefore sensitive), the impact these items requiring correction will have on the project if not corrected, and the anticipated time within which corrections can be expected.

The information contained in the vendor surveys may not always be complimentary to the vendor surveyed. Professionalism dictates that the report be marked company confidential, and that distribution be very limited. A file copy for SQA and one copy to the procurement manager should be sufficient distribution. *In no circumstance should the information about one vendor be given to any other vendor surveyed.*

The program manager will be required to make a selection decision based on the information available to his staff. The vendor survey information, and the associated cost impacts to the project, will be critical in that decision process. The vendor survey and report should therefore always be considered as a highly important and sensitive task, and one which may be of great importance to the vendor in maintaining or improving its business position. The SQA representative should always consider the impact of the report on the vendor, even though the report must of necessity be driven by the needs of the company performing the survey. This is why the maximum possible degree of objectivity is so important. If the SQA report is ever challenged, the validity of the results will be much more easily explained where the report is highly objective in the scoring technique.

During the internal decision conferences, SQA should be ready to assist the evaluation team in making its final decision. This may require some judgment as to the reasonableness of the vendor proposed cost as well as the technical merits of the vendor's SQA program.

Subcontractor Statement of Work

In every case where there is a subcontractor, the prime contractor has to issue a statement of work. This, in essence, is the contract document between the prime contractor and the subcontractor which defines the work to be done and the requirements, including quality requirements, which must be met. The subcontractor statement of work (SOW) should always provide for the flow-down of all of the applicable quality and other standards which have been imposed on the prime contractor. The subcontractor SOW should never be issued without being reviewed by SQA, and SQA should aways provide input to the SOW for those instances where any software development is being done by the subcontractor.

The question then becomes one of content. How much should be said in the SOW? How much detail should be included? A review of some actual case examples will illustrate the problem.

Case 1: Company A has selected Company B to provide parts and related software for a new personal computer. Company A has told Company B to provide information, on the display, for the user in the event of a problem. In full compliance with the SOW, Company B provides the information in a form such that when a problem occurs, a message appears on the display screen which reads, "ABEND XXX, LOCATION YYYYY." Company A tells Company B that this is not satisfactory and that the message must be user-friendly. Upon inquiry, Company B is told that user-friendly means that an ordinary person, not a computer professional, will have to respond to the message, and virtually none of those people have any idea what an ABEND means, and have no way to access the location or to do anything about it. It is information which cannot be responded to by the person receiving the information. So, Company B works on the message, and the next time it appears it says, "TAKE IT DOWN MAC; YOU'RE SUCKING MUD." The Company A contracts administrator explained that this was not exactly what he had in mind, although it was more informative than the first message.

Case 2: Company A has Company B under subcontract. The SOW provides that Company B will perform design and code inspections. Initial orientation is provided on the inspection process. However, nothing in the contract states the manner in which inspections would be done, or even defines inspections. When the contract work proceeds, the inspections are initially attended by Company A personnel and it is noted that the inspections are being conducted in the most cost-ineffective manner possible. The inspections are an all-day affair, with as many as 40 people coming in and out all day. It turns out they are a total waste of time and money. The Company A SQA representative discovers that the real inspections, more informal than desired and ones where no real analysis data is being collected, happen two to three days before so the code could be cleaned up before the public inspections, and that the big show is for the benefit of Company A personnel. Not very effective.

In both of these examples, the question is what should have been included in the statement of work? There has to be a balance between telling the subcontractor what to do, and telling them how to do it. The prime contractor must tell them what to do, including keeping files of objective evidence of SQA activity which is subject to audit by the prime contractor. What is not specified is not contractually obligated to be done. The "How" is where it gets touchy. Companies have a strong aversion to others telling them how to do their job, and rightly so. This is a problem which has been argued for years whenever new government standards are written. It is a very sensitive issue. It is an issue which SQA has to be aware of when providing input to the subcontractor SOW.

SQA input must specify what has to be done. It also must specify "How," provided it is necessary to do so. For example, if design and code inspections are to be required, it makes no sense to state that, and nothing more. Inspections are not a process used by everyone, and not everyone is familiar with the conduct of the inspections and data collection. Therefore, when inspections are required, and if SQA knows that the subcontractor is not particularly familiar with the inspection process, then some form of "How" information is required.

If a document is available on how inspections are to be done, and how the data is to be collected and reported, this document can be referenced and made a contractually binding document. Otherwise, the necessary information will have to be included in the body of the SOW. SQA will have to be mindful of what this means to a company not familiar with the process. For example, the subcontractor will have to budget for doing inspections, and may not know how, or what to include. SQA will usually not be allowed to tell them. This is because SQA cannot give contract direction to a company, and if SQA tells them it should cost a certain amount, and it costs a different amount, then Company A likely will have to absorb any additional cost, or may overspend unnecessarily.

If the subcontractor budgets to do the job for a certain amount, then that is all the subcontractor is entitled to receive for that work.

SQA should be particularly sensitive to phone calls asking for information about any requested items, especially if the question involves cost or any information which can be interpreted as cost information. If the SQA representative is not sure how or whether to respond, the issue should be set aside or the conversation should be politely terminated, and the matter discussed with the SQA department manager or contract administrator. A follow-up call should then always be made from a Company A contracts representative to the subcontractor with an answer.

SQA should support the program manager during contract negotiations. When the subcontractor submits the cost proposal, SQA should review the subcontractor SQA cost elements for reasonableness compared to what SQA included in the SOW and should provide this data to the program manager or contracts administrator. SQA should never interface directly with the subcontractor at this stage of the contract without express direction from the program manager or the contract administrator.

The bottom line is that when SQA provides input to the SOW, what is to be done must be included. Whether or not how it should be done is included, depends on the tasks being required and the knowledge base of the subcontractor. There is no clear-cut answer for this question. SQA ultimately has to consider that the subcontractor will be audited by SQA against the contents of the SOW, and if that content is being satisfied then SQA has no right to complain.

One final word of caution on this topic should be mentioned. One of the most common phrases found in contracts or statements of work, in the section on standards being invoked, is one which, in effect, states that "Standard 123-456 is imposed, to the extent specified herein." That little phrase, "to the extent specified herein" should be examined with considerable care. It flows up to the higher level documents and forms a chain of imposition which must be carefully scrutinized. It is a small phrase which is usually added without any thought, probably because someone on the last contract did so, or because it is part of the contract document generation boilerplate. But if the document is not "specified herein" in the SOW, then it is not a binding document even if it is in the list of applicable documents in the front of the SOW or prime contract. It is a phrase which I recommend deleting. Another actual case example is provided to illustrate why deletion is recommended.

Case 3: Company A lets a subcontract to Company B. The chain of documents, from the prime item specification on down, all refer to a particular software government standard, MIL-STD-1679. All contain the language, "to the extent specified herein" wherever the standard is mentioned in the list of reference documents. The provisions of the standard flow throughout the software chain of documents. However, one document, the prime contractor software functional requirements specification, does not mention the standard by name anywhere in the document, even though the basic provisions of the standard are included. The subcontractor SOW documents impose MIL-STD-1679, and do so within the body of the document by specific reference, but do so "as specified in the software functional requirements." The subcontractor refused to adhere to MIL-STD-1679, arguing that it was not a requirement on them. It was only the threat of the loss of follow-on business that made them agree to follow the standard. This could have gotten much worse, since the prime contractor was responsible for delivering the final composite product to the government in accordance with the prime contract, and might not have been able to do so if the subcontractor had not produced product in accordance with the required standard. SQA must be particularly aware of these kinds of issues when writing input for and reviewing any requirements for any subcontractor SOW.

SQA Initial Subcontractor Audits

A subcontractor can reach that status in basically three ways:

- the company can be a potential vendor and go through a competitive process to obtain the subcontract *or*
- the company can be part of a teaming agreement in submitting a proposal *or*
- the company can be sole source selected to provide a particular product or service.

It would be a grievous mistake to assume that, just because the subcontractor falls into either of the latter two situations, there is no need to perform an initial SQA audit as soon as the contract is signed, or even before.

Case 1: *Situation:* Company A is a large prime contractor for the government. They want to subcontract out part of a job, and select Company B as a subcontractor (how the selection process took place is not important to the point of this example). SQA initiates a request for travel authorization to complete an SQA audit. The product assurance manager for Company A refuses, giving as the reason that Company B is the best at what they do, and so even if problems are found, there is no one better qualified to do the job.

Error: The error in the product assurance manager's thinking is that even if Company B is the best, that does not mean they are able to meet the quality requirements of the contract. If any problems exist, they should be uncovered immediately so that they can be addressed at the beginning when it is the most efficacious time to do so.

Condition: Company B had never worked under the particular software MIL-STD before; the program manager and principal engineers all had hardware backgrounds; the contract standards required the use of high order languages (HOL) and the implementation of structured top-down programming and the Company B personnel did not understand how to do structured top-down programming; design and code inspections as described in Mike Fagan's paper[1] were required and Company B had never done inspections; Company B had no truly independent SQA department, SQA being totally controlled by the development organization; Company B had no independently implementable SQA written procedures, etc.

Result: The SQA audit was not performed. The previously described conditions were not detected early. When SQA finally was allowed to do a proper SQA audit, the situation had so deteriorated that it took over 18 months, and the removal of the Company A product assurance manager from that slot, to begin to address the situation.

Company B's suggestion for addressing the structured programming problem was to send one of their programmers to class for one week and have that programmer return to teach the other programmers (this suggestion was wisely negated by Company A).

The end result was that a 43 percent overrun was being projected by the time of the critical design review (CDR), and the only way to address the quality issues (not to mention technical issues) was for companies A and B to develop a "tailoring agreement" which literally watered the standards down to nothing, and involved the customer in that process. The customer representative involved was not a contracting officer but a technical administrator. The tailoring document signed by the customer technical administrator was therefore not binding on the government, but by that time the whole situation had become so embarrassing that everyone did what they thought would be best for the project and tried to ignore the rest. It was a management nightmare and did little to enhance the image of Company A as an effective subcontractor manager.

If an effective SQA audit had been conducted at the beginning, the conditions described would have been uncovered, the problems could have been addressed at the beginning when it would have been easiest and most cost-effective to do so. The situation could have been addressed without bringing the end customer into the picture and thereby embarrassing everyone, including the customer, and the projected cost overruns could have been addressed early in the contract life, and probably avoided altogether.

For situations where there was a lack of skill base, such as in structured programming, there could have been several actions taken, including timely and effective instruction being provided by Company A.

Or consider this situation:

Case 2: Company A is prime contractor on a large project where there are multiple other subcontractors, all large companies. The subcontractors are part of a proposal team arrangement, and so there is no vendor selection process once the team is identified. Initial SQA audits are done on two of the subcontractors after the prime contract is won. The subcontractors are obligated by contract to perform design and code inspections, and Company A agrees to provide initial orientation for this process at no cost to the subcontractors.

During the first SQA audit of Company B after the work has begun, Company A's SQA representative asks to see the inspection data results. The response from the Company B QA manager is "No." The rationale is that Company A said that inspections had to be done, but nothing required Company B to provide the data. If Company A wants the data, they can pay for it. The real reason was that Company B was concerned about the data being used by Company A as a tracking mechanism for evaluating Company B. Once this issue was resolved, the open communication established between the SQA departments at Company A and Company B was such that the Company B SQA program was continuously evaluated as one of the best. The communication assured it stayed that way. Whenever any question arose at either company, it was brought up and resolved immediately, before it could become a serious problem.

On the other hand, when Company C, another subcontractor on the same program, was evaluated, there was much to be desired in the way of an SQA program. There were no written SQA procedures, the task was undermanned, the experience level of the SQA personnel was quite low, and there was minimal, if any, support of the SQA function by the program manager. SQA had virtually no recognized and accepted authority to enforce any of the contractually imposed software quality requirements.

Company C SQA personnel wanted to do a good job, and had a fairly good idea of what to do, but were frustrated at every turn. The situation worsened with the next two audits, and finally the Company A SQA representative had to play the bad-guy role by issuing a failed audit report and requiring correction within a short time.

When there was no visible attempt to correct, the Company A SQA representative issued a formal notice to the Company A program manager that no more product would be accepted until the situation was corrected. This got the required level of attention, and, after several months, and the re-assignment of several managers, the fundamental issues of the situation were fairly well corrected. However, it took so long that other problems had arisen in the meantime and the result was something less than warm relations between the companies. The Company

A SQA representative should have pushed the issue a lot harder right from the beginning instead of allowing so much time for Company B's SQA department to try to correct their own situation. The bad-guy role was effective and should have been used much sooner. Since Company C's SQA department had so little clout, the Company A representative should have used all of the authority granted under the contract and the government standards applicable on the contract to push the issue immediately.

Regular Subcontractor Audits

The prime contractor SQA should audit the subcontractor on a regular basis. The audits should be scheduled and planned for, unless there is some condition which warrants an unscheduled audit. The prime contractor SQA should use the subcontractor SQA as the prime point of contact, and should audit the subcontractor SQA first during each audit trip.

In addition to the SQA department, the prime contractor SQA may audit the subcontractor software development department, the software configuration management department, or other software departments. These audits are part of the prime contractor SQA responsibility to assure that all provisions of the imposed standards are met, and that means that the provisions for software development, configuration management, and others, must be shown to have been met.

Whether or not the other departments are audited, is discretionary with the prime contractor SQA, but the subcontractor SQA should be audited every time, scheduled or otherwise. The degree to which the subcontractor SQA is able to perform, and is in fact performing, its required tasks is a major determinant in how extensively other subcontractor departments are audited by the prime contractor SQA representative. The tasks performed, and the objective evidence retained, will be major items in making these determinations.

A word of caution should be offered here to those conducting subcontractor audits on government programs, or other programs involving third parties. The subcontract defines a legal relationship between the prime contractor and the subcontractor. The procuring agency, such as the government, is not a party to the subcontract even though the product will eventually be delivered to the government. The product is delivered to the third party procuring agency (government) by the prime contractor, not the subcontractor, and the prime contractor is the only party with responsibility to the government.

When the prime contractor SQA is auditing the subcontractor, the only parties present should be the prime contractor SQA and the personnel from the subcontractor. Occasionally, other parties, such as the government DCAS representative, or any other interested third party, may ask to attend the audit, or even demand they be allowed to attend. The prime contractor SQA should politely, but firmly, refuse to allow this without the contracting officers of *both* companies agreeing in advance. The government is not a party to the contract and has no business attending the audit between the two companies.

Not all DCAS representatives understand this, and some may get quite upset, but any amount of bluster possible is not sufficient reason to allow a third party to participate in the private contractual activities between the two companies. When the audit report is filed as objective evidence, DCAS will have plenty of opportunity to review the report. If they need training on conducting software audits, this is not the forum to provide that training.

The frequency of audits of the subcontractor is best computed as a function of the development's life cycle. The audits should be conducted at major milestones. They should be conducted at intermediate milestone points if a life cycle phase is long in relation to others, or if considerable critical activity is taking place. The schedule of planned audits should be published, and should show audits being conducted at least twice a year, preferably quarterly. It can, of course, be modified as the needs of the project dictate.

Upon completion of every audit of the subcontractor, the prime contractor SQA should hold a debriefing meeting with the subcontractor program manager and the SQA manager. The results of the audit should be discussed, as well as a list of any action items which require attention and their due dates. This should be recorded in a set of minutes and the subcontractor program manager and SQA representative should receive copies. The minutes need not be typed, and can be completed, and initialed by all parties, prior to the prime contractor SQA representative leaving the facility. A copy of the minutes should be provided to the prime contractor contract administrator and program manager, and a formal copy sent from the prime contractor contract administrator to the subcontractor contract administrator.

The audit action items should be tracked carefully and reported at regular program review meetings. Any action required should be taken to assure a quick resolution. The longer an item is on the action item list without any activity, the harder it will be to begin activity. Any item open for more than two weeks should be tracked at the prime contractor weekly program review meetings. If it lies dormant for too long, it is presumed to be unimportant. After all, if it is important, why isn't the prime contractor SQA screaming about it?

A variety of actions can be taken to correct deficiencies uncovered in audits. The simplest is to note the existence of the problem and obtain commitment from the subcontractor to make the correction. The prime contractor SQA should impose a time limit, and require that it be notified when the correction is effected. The most drastic action is to refuse to accept product until the condition is corrected. There are many shades of gray in between.

If the latter action is taken, a certain level of heat is generated and there should be good, documented reason for the action. This step should be taken only in a case where there is a condition of non-compliance with a contract requirement, and the prime contractor will be subject to audit for that item. Remember, especially if it is a government contract, if you charge for an item (and an item can be a task as well as a physical object), it is fraud not to provide it. It is taking funds for performing a task which is not performed. It is not something to be taken lightly. If your name is on the line as the SQA representative stating that an audit has been performed and the subcontractor is in compliance with the quality requirements of the contract, there better not be any reason for the customer to believe that you are sweeping matters under the rug just to placate your own program manager or to avoid making waves. If making waves bothers you, get out of the SQA business.

Subcontractor Internal SQA Activity

The prime contractor SQA should require any subcontractor to engage in certain fundamental activity. This activity is auditable, provided the subcontractor is required to keep the proper kinds of objective evidence.

Subcontractor SQA Plans

The subcontractor SOW should provide for certain deliverable items, including a subcontractor SQA plan (SQAP) and software quality evaluation plan (SQEP). If the option is provided for the subcontractor SQA to adopt the prime contractor SQA plan as its own, a qualification document should be required which will denote any changes, deletions or additions. It is quite rare for any well-written SQA plan for a particular company, considering the development methods used and the organizational structure of that company, to be totally applicable to another company without modification.

The SQA plan should be required to document in detail the SQA procedures which will be followed on the contract. In lieu of this, a procedures manual can be incorporated by reference in the SQA plan, as long as a copy is provided to the prime contractor SQA for review (watch out for "to the extent specified herein/therein/etc."). Where documentation standards are governing the contract, the requirements of the standard for the SQA plan must be followed.

The subcontractor SQA plan must adhere to the provisions of the SOW, and must incorporate procedures which will provide for assuring that all of the provisions of the contractually imposed standards are followed. How this is done is a subcontractor decision, as long as the record of what is done is kept on file and is auditable, and as long as the method used is effective as to the requirements of the contract.

Subcontractor Document Review

The subcontractor SQA department should review every software deliverable document for adherence to the contract's requirements. This always should be done before the document is delivered to the prime contractor. The subcontractor SQA should review the document in draft, note any discrepancies, and require correction in the final draft before delivery to the prime contractor.

The prime contractor should require that the subcontractor SQA review and approve every deliverable software document prior to delivery to the prime contractor. For each document reviewed, the subcontractor SQA should record the fact of the review and approval for objective evidence. The prime contractor should also require that evidence of the review be displayed prominently on the cover page of the document. This can be in the form of a stamp or other such indicator, with an accept/reject indication, and an indication of the reviewer's identity. This is an indication that the subcontractor SQA is certifying to the prime contractor that the document meets the contract's documentation standards. If there is no such indication, the prime contractor should immediately reject and return the document as non-conforming with the contract. After all, there is no reason why the prime contractor should have to do a documentation standard review of a subcontractor-delivered document. That is a task for which the subcontractor SQA is being paid.

Subcontractor Internal Audits

The subcontractor SQA plan (SQAP) and subcontractor software quality evaluation plan (SQEP) should provide for internal audits of the subcontractor activity by the subcontractor SQA, and should include audits of all software-related functions active on the contract, including software configuration management. The frequency should be specified and copies of any checklists used should be included as an appendix to the SQAP or SQEP. Provision should be made for the retention of objective evidence of all audit activity, and the objective evidence is subject to audit by the prime contractor. Following each audit there should be an audit report. The audit reports also should be kept on file by SQA and are subject to audit by the prime contractor SQA.

The software corrective action program and procedures, including document corrective action and software process corrective action, should be described in the subcontractor SQAP or SQEP, or in the deliverable software development plan, and should provide for effective SQA involvement. SQA should keep on file, subject to audit, records of the activity related to corrective action. This may be in the form of document review records, PTR trend charts, inspection process data analysis, and the like.

If there is any problem of responsiveness from those audited by the subcontractor SQA, the SQA plan should provide for a program, approved by the subcontractor management team, of escalation of the issue to a level of management where the problem is resolved. This record is also subject to audit.

The auditability of the SQA records is not for the purpose of looking into the subcontractor's "dirty laundry," but is a required part of the prime contractor SQA function. The prime contractor SQA is required, on government contracts, to assure to the government that all of the provisions of the contract standards are adhered to. Audits are one of the provisions of these standards, and if the subcontractor is doing a portion of the contract work, the prime contractor SQA is obligated by contract to assure, and must certify to the government, that this internal audit provision is being met.

Program Reviews

The prime contractor should require that at all program review meetings, usually held monthly or bimonthly, a subcontractor SQA status report is given. This status report should include the status of the SQA activity and address all open action items. It should include the status of SQA review of contract deliverable documents, the status of any software defect detection and removal processes, the status of program trouble reports (PTRs), the status of internal audits conducted, and other SQA-related actions. This information should be included in the program review's minutes.

Subcontractor Test Activity

The subcontractor SQA involvement in internal test activity should mirror that of the prime contractor, provided there is a similar effective early defect detection and removal process. This last point is the primary operative phrase. Early defect detection and removal does not mean beginning at unit test, or after. It means to begin as soon as the generation process begins—at the requirements level. Since this will vary to a considerable extent from company to company, the degree of test activity involvement required by the subcontractor SQA will be dependent upon the degree to which that company relies on the test phases as a primary defect removal activity. The prime contractor SQA will have to be sensitive to this in determining the effectiveness of, and evaluating, the subcontractor SQA program.

During final acceptance test, the subcontractor SQA should be a witness for the entire test, and should have the same responsibilities as described for the prime contractor SQA in Chapter 7. At the acceptance test, the prime contractor will have a representative. This may be SQA and/or a technical expert. The subcontractor SQA should be able to answer any questions raised about the software's status, the integrity of the software tested, where it has been kept, from which library it has been generated, how it will be delivered, and what SQA delivery checks will be provided. Upon delivery, each piece of software media delivered should be bonded by the subcontractor SQA before it leaves the subcontractor facility. Any product not so bonded should be rejected as unacceptable by the prime contractor. It is a question of accountability, not how well the product will work if it is not bonded.

Note

1. Fagan, M. E., "Design and Code Inspections to Reduce Errors in a Program Development." *IBM Systems Journal*, No. 3 (July 1976), pp. 182–207.

CHAPTER 9

GOVERNMENT QUALITY AUDIT ACTIVITY AND AUTHORITY

Government Quality Assurance Organization Interface

One of the most important relationships SQA will have for government projects is that which it establishes with the government quality assurance personnel, such as the Defense Contract Administration Service (DCAS), and similar service agencies, including AFPRO, ARPRO, and NAVPRO. When the term DCAS is used, it should be interpreted as including all these related organizations.

The DCAS organization is basically the government's SQA. DCAS comes under the chain of authority of the Defense Logistics Agency (DLA), headquartered in Cameron Station, Virginia. There is also an arm of the organization which concentrates primarily on financial audits. This is the Defense Contract Audit Activity (DCAA). The DCAA organization is the branch which will, for example, audit contractor cost proposals.

DCAS is responsible for evaluating the contractor's quality program. Often, where there is a large volume of government business, there may be a DCAS organization on-site with the contractor. If the activity is large enough, DCAS may have a plant representative's office (PRO), referred to as DCASPRO, resident at the contractor facility.

The remainder of this discussion will concentrate on the SQA/DCAS interface, since SQA representatives seldom, if ever, have contact with the DCAA office. The information provided here will be equally applicable to the service organizations such as AFPRO, ARPRO or NAVPRO (Air Force, Army and Navy, respectively). This discussion assumes there are software-conversant DCAS individuals performing the activities described.

DCAS Audits

The DCAS organization generally will have individuals assigned for evaluation of the hardware and software quality assurance process at a contractor's site. For software, DCAS will perform two fundamental actions. They will audit SQA for adherence to their procedures, and they will conduct an in-process audit of the software development organizations.

The DCAS SQA procedures evaluation (PE) is conducted by DCAS as an audit of the SQA department. It is exactly what its name implies—it is a procedures audit. It is an audit of the procedures developed by SQA and the manner in which SQA has adhered to its published procedures. DCAS is granted authority to perform the inspections by virtue of the provisions of government quality documents (MIL-Q and MIL-S), and the Defense Logistics Agency Manual (DLAM) 8200.1. MIL-Q-9858 and MIL-S-52779, in whatever nomenclature their most current version may take, have been the DCAS's guidance for a long time.

MIL-S-52779 is the software equivalent of MIL-Q-9858. Upon the approval of DoD-STD-2168, the government agreed that MIL-Q-9858 will not apply to software.

The fundamental provisions of MIL-S-52779 are:

- Documented SQA program must be in place.
- Fully documented SQA procedures.
- Program is subject to customer disapproval.
- Work tasks must be documented and authorized.
- Development schedules must be in place.
- SQA program must provide procedures to:
    - **Detect** software deficiencies.
    - **Report** software deficiencies.
    - **Analyze** software deficiencies.
    - **Correct** software deficiencies.

There must also be a provision for preventing unauthorized access to, and modification of software resident in controlled libraries.

A big drawback to MIL-S-52779 is that the base document is so old. For example, MIL-S-52779(A):

- Does not mandate modern software practices.
- Gives no guidance on software evaluation.
- Gives no guidance on evaluation of new practices.
- Does not define software quality with sufficient particularity for evaluator to make judgment.
- Does not list attributes of quality software.

It is quite difficult for DCAS, especially in the current situation with DoD-STD-2167A and DoD-STD-2168, to use MIL-S-52779 as a guiding document in evaluating a contractor's software quality evaluation program. This is why DoD-STD-2168 supersedes MIL-S-52779(A).

Even when the MIL-S-52779 requirements were combined with the requirements of some of the more current software development standards, such as DoD-STD-1679A, there was not sufficient guidance. For example:
Combined 52779(A) and 1679A requirements:

- Requires documented quality planning.
- Requires "assuring" that others do certain tasks:
  - Through audits.
  - Through product reviews.
  - Through process reviews.
- Requires production of deliverable SQA plan.
- Mandates that SQA assure all requirements of 1679A are followed, including:
  - Documentation review.
  - Test witnessing.

— Non-conformance reporting.

— Software media control.

— DCAS/DCASPRO interface.

— Subcontractor interface.

The fundamental flavor of the government standards prior to DoD-STD-2167 had been one of placing SQA in a police role. This is the role in which SQA found itself several years ago, and in which it still finds itself in some locations. However, in the current situations where SQA still has the police authority, but is actively putting into practice processes, procedures and techniques which are contributory, and which prevent the conditions requiring police action, then the older standards are not sufficient for DCAS evaluation of an SQA software quality evaluation program.

The contractor always can say the DCAS problem of evaluating a quality program is not his business, but that does not accomplish much. The contractor also can establish effective communication with DCAS, and inform DCAS of the activities being conducted, why they are conducted, and how, and thereby establish an effective working relationship. It gives DCAS the information they need to begin the evaluation process, but does so without placing DCAS in an awkward position where they might be subject to criticism for not doing a proper evaluation, or being in the contractor's pocket.

The DCAS audits of SQA are preceded by a review of the contract quality requirements (including the standards in place, however they might have been tailored during negotiations), a review of the SQA procedures manual, and a review of the contract SQA plan or contract software quality evaluation plan. DCAS will establish an audit checklist (DD Form 1709) to use in performing the PE. A similar review precedes the DCAS audit of any of the other contractor software departments. Each review will require a separate DD Form 1709.

DCAS Objective

It is important to understand that both SQA and DCAS are trying to assure that the same thing is accomplished. They really are on the same side. Both have the objective, and responsibility, to assure that the product is delivered to the government in conformance with the quality requirements present on the contract. DCAS is also concerned with ineffective practices which do nothing except cost money without adding value to the contract. This should also be an SQA concern. There are provisions of some standards which can, if interpreted literally, lead to such a condition. For example, some ineffective practices and cost drivers of MIL-STD-1679:

- Code-walkthrough *before* compile:
  - — inefficient.
- SQA to witness *all* tests:
  - — Have been interpreted literally.
  - — Huge cost if implemented literally.
  - — No real value for cost expended.
- Specified STR reporting system, with forms:
  - — Only effective if contractor has no system, or if system in place is deficient.

When DCAS performs a PE, they look for implementation of the contract requirements through published procedures established by the contractor. For each requirement, there should be a procedure and also objective evidence showing that the procedure has been followed. The PE is a major tool of the DCAS in-process inspection activity.

Audit Criteria and Frequency

DCAS audits are based on the checklist developed for that contract, and for the department being audited. Each item in the checklist has a separate nomenclature. These checklist items are referred to as characteristics. During the initial PE, all checklist characteristics are inspected. After the initial PE, the frequency at which DCAS will audit a particular characteristic will depend on such factors as the consistency of compliance with that requirement, the history of non-compliance, or the criticality of that item. The audits may be performed every 30 days, but any given characteristic may be audited on up to a 90-day schedule. Therefore, even though DCAS may do an audit every 30 days, that does not mean every characteristic is audited every 30 days. The frequency of inspection for some items is specified by government regulation, and for others it is up to the discretion of the person conducting the audit.

Scope of PE

All contractor organizations are subject to DCAS audit. Each organization is audited for compliance with the various work instructions which are on record. The organizations audited might include SQA, configuration management, software test, system engineering, or any other group involved in the software development process. DCAS will look for organization connections and dependencies that might lead to decisions which favor schedule or cost over quality. DCAS has no concern with the cost of any action. That is the contractor's problem. If a given characteristic is required by the contract, DCAS will expect it to be provided.

DCAS Non-Conformance Reports

When DCAS performs audits using DD Form 1709, the required characteristics are listed and audited for compliance. DD Form 1709 has two major portions. One is where DCAS records, verbatim, a contractor statement contained in one of the documents reviewed. For example, the Software Development Plan might have stated that every program module will have a unique diagram showing the structure and constructs, and identifying the levels of nested code within the module. The second part of the DD Form 1709 will state the method used by DCAS to evaluate this characteristic.

The result of the audit will be recorded on the DD Form 1709, or on an Observation Record, DD Form 1711.

Non-conformances are documented on a government form and the resultant non-conformance report is referred to as a method. There are five possibilities: Method A, Method B, Method C, Method D, and Method E.

A *Method A* corrective action means the deficiency was corrected immediately during the audit. No further action is required.

A *Method B* really is the first level of method utilized as a result of a PE, and is recorded on a DD Form 1715. This is the familiar Quality Deficiency Record (QDR). It, in essence, says that there is a contract quality requirement which is not being met. The contractor has a specified number of days in which to respond and implement corrective action. The corrective action is expected to include a statement of what has been done to preclude the same problem from occurring again.

If a Method B is not responded to adequately, or within a reasonable time, the Method B (QDR) is escalated to the executive manager of the function audited and it then becomes a *Method C.* If a positive corrective action is not received at this level, DCAS will issue a *Method D,* which in effect shuts the doors of the plant. When a Method D is issued, the government stops accepting product from the contractor and the contractor receives no further payment for the products produced.

A *Method E* is issued when a subcontractor has QDRs issued which have escalated to the Method C level. The Method E is sent to the prime contractor and, in essence, says that the prime contractor has done a poor job managing the subcontractor and requires that the prime contractor initiate corrective action. It is a lead-in to the issuance of a Method D to the prime contractor because of the conditions present at a subcontractor location. The prime contractor cannot deliver product to the government which comes from a subcontractor who has been issued a Method D.

DCAS Communication

The more effective the communication between the DCAS organization and the contractor SQA organization, the more smoothly the process will work. It has been shown from experience that where there is regular and effective interface between DCAS and the contractor, the number of problems which escalate to the QDR level, and beyond, are minimal.

One of the most effective processes so far has been the establishment of regular DCAS/contractor meetings where the status of ongoing activity is discussed and where any issues of concern can be raised early and addressed effectively. If the contractor is open and keeps DCAS informed, the ability to identify and address problems early is significantly enhanced, and the need for the issuance of Method B or Method C corrective actions is minimized or eliminated. It does not remove any independence from the DCAS operation (in fact, that must be preserved at all times), but opens the lines of communication for effective activity toward their common goal.

The DCAS/contractor SQA meetings should be frequent, especially at first when effective communication is being established. The meetings should begin at a frequency of one per week, and perhaps later changed to twice a month. All SQA/DCAS-related issues should be discussed, including the scheduling of any PE, any concerns or questions DCAS might have, any changes to the SQA procedures which SQA is planning, any problems which DCAS or SQA is anticipating, and similar issues. Minutes of the meetings should be kept and copied to those in attendance and to the respective managers. It also is often quite effective for the SQA department to establish one individual as the primary interface with DCAS for these meetings. Often this will help both organizations to assure that items of interest do not get lost. This in no way should interfere with the right of DCAS to interface with any SQA contract representative at any time. The prime interface is an expeditor, not a blockade.

CHAPTER 10

STANDARDS AND SPECIFICATIONS: MILITARY AND INDUSTRY

Military Standards and Specifications

The military standards which have been governing weapon system contracts in the past have been, primarily, MIL-STD-1679, DoD-STD-1679A, MIL-STD-1644, MIL-STD-483, MIL-STD-490, and MIL-STD-1521. Many contracts remain ongoing where these standards were invoked, and therefore they are still governing on those contracts. This is so even though DoD-STD-1679A superseded MIL-STD-1679, and DoD-STD-2167 has superseded DoD-STD-1679A, and DoD-STD-2167A has superseded DoD-STD-2167. The specifications which have been governing software have primarily been MIL-Q-9858 and MIL-S-52779. MIL-S-52779 has been superseded by DoD-STD-2168.

MIL-STD-1679/DoD-STD-1679A/ DoD-STD-2167/DoD-STD-2167A

The chain of standards MIL-STD-1679, DoD-STD-1679A, DoD-STD-2167, and DoD-STD-2167A are software development standards, not quality assurance standards. The 1679 series documents have incorporated within them software quality assurance provisions, as well as provisions for other software development-related activity, including configuration management, software test, and program management.

Comparison between DoD-STD-1679A and DoD-STD-2167

DoD-STD-2167 is the successor to DoD-STD-1679A. When it was published, there also was published a comparison study between the provisions of DoD-STD-1679A and DoD-STD-2167. There was great commonality of intent, but there were also some interesting differences, especially from an SQA point of view.

Paragraph 4.4 of 1679A required that SQA "plan, develop, and implement procedures and practices to ensure that *all* requirements of the contract, including this standard, are complied with fully." The comparable provision of DoD-STD-2167, found in paragraph 4.3.c, "requires the contractor to establish and maintain a process to evaluate the software, associated documentation, and the software development process. . . . The quality evaluation process is to include both contractor internal steps specified in the SDP (Software Development Plan) or SQEP (Software Quality Evaluation Plan) and the formal steps specified in 5.8."

In addition, 2167 requires that the evaluation be carried out by those having the expertise to do so and organizational independence from the function evaluated. In short, it does not require a centralized SQA function for performance of the evaluations, and does not require that SQA itself assure compliance with *all* of the standard's provisions.

The standard is specifically written to be tailored. In addition, 2167 does not require particular evaluation techniques (whereas 1679A specifically required assessments, document reviews, design reviews, walk-throughs, monitoring, auditing, and testing), and does not specifically mandate testing as a part of the Software Quality Evaluation Program. It requires internal in-process reviews. The review's results are to be incorporated prior to presenting the document to the contracting agency (paragraphs 5.2.3 and 5.3.3).

SQA also should be aware that whereas 1679A prohibits GO-TO statements, 2167 does not address this issue specifically, although the data item descriptions (DIDs) would imply this prohibition. But 2167 does require top-down design, code and test, and requires the contractor to follow approved coding standards.

Another significant difference from the SQA perspective, which should be considered carefully in developing the subcontractor SOW, is that 1679A required that the prime contractor quality requirements flow down to subcontractors, whereas 2167 requires only that the contractor ensure that all subcontractors comply with the subcontract requirements (paragraph 4.5). Therefore, there is no automatic flow-down of the standard to subcontractors. In addition, 2167 requires that the subcontractor delivered products shall be evaluated for completeness, technical adequacy and compliance with subcontract requirements (paragraph 5.8.1.6). However, 2167 (in paragraph 4.11) also states that the subcontractor shall develop software in compliance with this standard, as required by the contract, unless a deviation or waiver has been approved.

Please note that here is another of the phrases which are in the general class of "to the extent specified herein" discussed in

Chapter 8. It is buried right in the middle of the sentence ("as required by the contract") in the standard itself.

SQA must be particularly careful of the chain of activating phrases and included requirements in the succeeding documents. This makes SQA's review of, and input to, the subcontract SOW all the more important. Be aware that not including the requirement of compliance with 2167 in the SOW is tantamount to a blanket waiver of the standard for that subcontract. If it is imposed in the prime contract, and not included in the subcontract, the prime contractor may have considerable difficulty in meeting its own delivery requirements.

SQA also should be sensitive to the levels of specificity in the standards as they change. In 1679A, there is a specific prohibition against recursive code. In 2167, there is no comparable specific statement, but the Data Item Description (DID) for the Software Top Level Design Document (STLDD), DID DI-MCCR-80012, and the Software Detailed Design Document (SDDD), DID DI-MCCR-80031, appear to have this requirement included. Again, SQA must be able to evaluate this requirement, or assure that it has been evaluated.

In 1679A, there is a requirement for verification of the architecture. The standard specifically states that the verification "may require extensive modeling, prototyping, or simulation, and shall in all cases be completed prior to design implementation." In 2167, the requirement is not nearly so explicit, the methods are not specified, and the requirement is spread out over at least five different paragraphs, specifically 5.2.1.11, 5.3.1.19, 5.3.1.7, 5.5.1.4, and 5.9.1.1.

These examples are provided to point out the necessity for SQA to perform a very detailed review of all of the requirements in the new standards, understand the implications of the different paragraphs which address the same or related issues, understand how and when a particular DID might clarify the standard, and understand the implications of the tailoring of any one phrase of the standard.

Tailoring

An important aspect of the SQA task is the ability to understand the implications of the tailoring process. DoD-STD-2167, DoD-STD-2167A, and DoD-STD-2168 were all written to be tailored. They are the first DoD software standards written with the specific intent that they be tailored for each contract.

If a given element of 2167 is tailored out, what is the result as far as quality requirements are concerned? For example, if the pertinent provisions of the STLDD regarding recursivity are tailored, but the corresponding provision in the SDDD is not tailored, what does this imply? Is recursivity allowed or forbidden?

In a standards tailoring environment, the SQA task will be much more complicated than writing an SQA plan and passing it on to the customer. *The SQA task in recommending, and evaluating, any tailoring of the standard is an absolutely critical element of the SQA planning process.*

The tailoring guide provided as an appendix to DoD-STD-2167 is some help, as are the handbooks for DoD-STD-2167 and DoD-STD-2168, DoD *Handbook 287* and DoD *Handbook 288*, respectively. The courses offered by Dynamic Research Corporation (DRC) are also excellent sources of information and guidance. These DRC courses have been offered to the government personnel in various locations and at various levels of responsibility. Gramm-Rudman notwithstanding, DLA should make these courses mandatory for all DCAS personnel currently assigned, or to be assigned, responsibility as quality assurance representatives (QAR) on any software development contract.

It is interesting to note, when considering the progression of these standards, that MIL-STD-1644A, which is the trainer systems' equivalent of DoD-STD-1679A, has had no DoD-STD-2167 comparable counterpart development.

Compliance Matrix

In assessing the provisions of the new standards, DoD-STD-2167A and DoD-STD-2168, the SQA department should prepare a detailed cross-reference matrix wherein each provision of each paragraph is included, and referenced to the paragraph number. This matrix should include a cross-reference to every provision, every related provision elsewhere in the standard, every related provision of an appropriate DID, and any related provision of any companion standard, such as DoD-STD-2168.

The DoD-STD-2167A and DoD-STD-2168 Environment

DoD-STD-2167A and DoD-STD-2168 were written to respond to the needs of a changing environment. The objective was to develop tri-service standards which could be contributory in an environment where DoD will be spending twenty billion dollars annually on software, where there is a demand for increasing productivity and quality of software through automation, where there is a drive for technology insertion (as seen in Ada), and a need for streamlining the software standards directives.

The environment is one which includes:

- Rapidly evolving software technology.
- A wide variety of software engineering practices.
- Tri-service policy and service regulations.
- The evolvement of the STARS program.
- Activities of the Ada Joint Program Office.
- Programs of the Software Engineering Institute.
- The Defense Advanced Research Project Agency (DARPA) activity.
- The total quality management (TQM) and R&M 2000 activities.
- The industry activity in development of standards, such as those produced or adopted by IEEE and ANSI.

DoD-STD-2167A and DoD-STD-2168 were written to be both tailored and modified. DoD-STD-2167A has been published, and a revision B is in the initial planning stages. The development of these standards was an issue-based development. They were written to be responsive, not overbearing. The development of these standards has been one of the best examples of DoD and industry cooperation. The volume of review and input provided by industry, the activity of the CODSIA review groups, and the general acceptance of the documents in industry is a credit to this effort.

The planned progression of DoD-STD-2167 will move from the present day focus of a transition from DoD-STD-1679A, to a primary focus on the STARS requirements in revision C. Revision C is expected about 1991. Following this progression, the emphasis will shift to the advanced work being done by DARPA in very high level languages, artificial intelligence and neural networks. A revision to this level is targeted for the time period between 1995 and the year 2000. Therefore, this is an ongoing effort and is very responsive to the needs of both DoD and industry.

The DoD-STD-2167 is an attempt, at each revision level, to incorporate the state-of-the-practice. There is a working group set up to evaluate the differences between the state-of-the-practice and the state-of-the-art. There will be a gradual transition of state-of-the-art provisions into the standard as the state-of-the-art becomes state-of-the-practice.

There were five primary issues raised by the publication of DoD-STD-2167. They were:

- Adaptability to Ada.
- Tailoring.
- DID restructure and number.
- Control of the contractor's internal process.
- System engineering.

These issues are a matter of continuing review, and changes related to some of these issues were incorporated into the revision A of DoD-STD-2167 along with DoD-STD-2168.

Industry Standards

Industry, especially the IEEE Computer Society, headquartered in Washington, D.C., has been actively producing software standards and their related guides or recommended practices. Several standards already have been produced. Lists of the standards and their numbers are available from the IEEE Computer Society, or the IEEE Service Center in Piscataway, New Jersey. Several other standards, guides, or recommended practices are ongoing and are in various stages of completion. As of January 1, 1987, some of these ongoing projects are:

P982.1 *A Standard for Definitions of Measures to Produce Reliable Software (published May 1989)*
P982.2 *A Guide to a Standard for Definitions of Measures to Produce Reliable Software (published May 1989)*
P990 *A Guide to the Use of Ada as a PDL*
P1002 *A Standard for Software Engineering Standards Taxonomy.*
P1012 *A Standard for Software Verification and Validation Plans*
P1016 *A Guide for Software Design Descriptions*

P1028 *A Standard for Software Reviews and Audits*
P1042 *A Guide for Software Configuration Management*
P1044 *A Standard for Classification of Software Errors, Faults, and Failures*
P1045 *A Standard for Software Productivity Metrics*
P1058 *A Standard for Software Project Management Plans*
P1059 *A Guide for Software Verification and Validation*
P1060 *A Guide for Software Maintenance*
P1061 *A Standard for Software Quality Metrics*
P1062 *A Recommended Practice for Software Certification*
P1063 *A Standard for Software User Documentation*
P1074 *A Standard for Software Life Cycle Processes*

The creation of the documents is accomplished through the voluntary participation of people from all over the world. For example, the 982/982.1 documents were produced utilizing the talents of a group of over 300 professionals from both industry and government, and from almost every country in the free world. Notably absent was participation from South America and Africa.

The effort expended was considerable, with subcommittees formed to address all of the pertinent issues, including research into available metrics, selection of those measures pertinent to the issue of reliability management, editorial subcommittees, review of other standards already formed to assure there would be no conflicts, and others.

The production of an IEEE industry standard must be exactly that—an industry standard. It therefore cannot be written for a particular segment of the industry. The P982 standard, for example, had to be applicable to all of industry even though there were a number of participants from DoD and from DoD contractors. This led to a standard applicable to real time systems, non-real time systems, weapons systems, banking systems, nuclear industry systems, etc. Selecting the proper material to include in a standard addressing reliability where the application environments are so varied was not a trivial task by any means.

This was further complicated by the decision to do something really useful for the industry and not address only the issue of software reliability measurement. Confining the material only to the measurement of software reliability would have resulted in one more document(s) addressing the applicability of the known software reliability statistical models. There were already many such documents, some of them excellent, such as the study done by Dr. William Farr.[1]

What was needed was a way to manage reliability, through a measurement process, so that the reliability could be controlled throughout the development life cycle. This was the goal which was set for the 982.1/982.2 documents.

Similar kinds of activities are taking place with the other documents being developed. The joint government-industry involvement has had numerous benefits. Given the general acceptance of IEEE documents when published, the government often is specifying the IEEE standards as contractually binding documents. This is good, but the user must be aware of the nature of the documents specified. For example, the tailoring of DoD-STD-2167 and DoD-STD-2168 was discussed previously. The same is true for some of the IEEE standards; 982 must be tailored. It would be virtually impossible to try to apply the entire set of measures in the standard to a given project. Some of the measures included in that standard are product measures, while others are process-dependent measures. The user must select the measures most applicable to the particular environment and apply them.

The industry standards activity is open to participation by virtually anyone who wishes to become involved. The companies for which the volunteers work provide support for the activity of their people. The standards groups (such as IEEE) do not fund the working group activity. The working group meetings are held in various locations, depending on where the working group members are located. A member usually hosts the meeting at his or her location in order to eliminate the cost of renting a hotel conference room. This is part of the cost covered by the company supporting the participation of an employee. Those wishing to participate get authorization from their company, and then notify the working group chairperson of their desire to become involved.

There is already in place an approved IEEE standard for software quality assurance plans (IEEE/ANSI Standard 730). This document can be obtained directly from IEEE. This IEEE Standard 730 provides the acceptable minimal requirements for a software quality assurance plan, and therefore defines the activities which must be addressed, fundamentally, by any acceptable SQA function. If a software quality assurance department cannot meet the requirements of this basic standard, the problem is much deeper than might have been suspected.

The IEEE Standard 730, A Standard for Software Quality Assurance Plans, is now a joint IEEE/ANSI Standard. It was approved in 1981 by the IEEE Standards Board, and in 1982 by the American National Standards Institute (ANSI). This standard defines and describes each of the elements which should be included in an acceptable SQA plan. This does not mean that it was written to meet the format requirements of a government DID. It is written as an industry standard.

An SQA plan should be written for any software development project, whether the plan is deliverable or not. The scope of the IEEE standard, and the specified elements which are to be included in the plan, are those which would be found in any meaningful SQA activity.

There are numerous other IEEE standards available, including standards on terminology, configuration management, and software test documentation. There also is a guide to software quality assurance plans, IEEE Standard 983.

These standards are a rich source of information for any professional, and an invaluable source of guidance for anyone attempting to establish an SQA department or function, and who requires a basic and complete set of guiding standards to use as the starting point for the activity. With such guidance, the practitioner is not operating blindly. These documents contain the collective expertise of many professionals who have taken their time and contributed their talents to provide the industry with the needed guidance. There is no need to re-invent the wheel when this sort of guidance is available.

Note

1. Farr, W. H., "A Survey of Software Reliability Modeling and Estimation." Naval Surface Weapons Center, Dahlgren, Virginia, Technical Report TR82-171 (October 1983).

CHAPTER 11

SOFTWARE QUALITY EVALUATION—THE FUTURE

Software Quality Evaluation

The role of software quality assurance as we know it today will be viewed as a dinosaur by the mid 1990s. There is a strong shift of emphasis from the assurance that quality-related activities have taken place, to a requirement for evaluation and certification of the process and product quality during all life cycle phases. This will require a new kind of quality assurance and evaluation person for both the developers and the procuring agencies.

The developers no longer will be able to state that the correct things are being done to produce high quality products. They will have to evaluate themselves and prove and certify that this has been done. The results of the evaluation will be subject to procuring agency review. The certification will have both technical and legal implications.

There will be greater responsibilities on both sides. The developers will have a greater responsibility for correctly produced products, and the responsibility to prove it. The procuring agencies will have a much greater responsibility in assuring that the requirements for a system are firmly established early, and for assuring that minimal requirements changes are made. If any changes in requirements are proposed, the procuring agencies will have to justify the changes to themselves, as well as to the developer. Every change in requirements means work is redone, and work redone is always an impact to productivity. The procuring agencies have as much responsibility for high productivity development of a system as do the developers.

Government Quality Auditors

The government quality assurance auditors, such as DCAS, will have to become quite conversant with automated evaluation and analysis processes, and be able to assess the information provided by that environment. They will have to be able to understand the measurement processes, evaluate the evaluation programs and determine if those evaluation plans are sufficient to meet the procuring agency needs. This will require an extensive training process for all government personnel engaged in software quality evaluation activity. Such a training process appears to be much further in the future than the automated evaluation programs which are being and will be developed. If this actually is the situation, and if this is not corrected soon, then the procuring agencies will be behind the power curve in realizing that what they require is actually being provided.

Some individuals within the government have had the foresight to recognize this and have attempted to produce some fundamental direction in the form of basic documentation. The initial documents produced at the Air Force Systems Command Headquarters, in the form of AFSC Pamphlet 800–43 (*Software Management Indicators*), AFSC Pamphlet 800–14 (*Software Quality Indicators*), the AFSC Pamphlet 800–45 (*Software Risk Abatement*), and the draft AFSC Pamphlet 800–51 (*Pre-Award Survey*), are an excellent start, but are not a mandatory part of any DCAS training program. These documents should form the basis for a mandatory training program for all DCAS personnel. In addition, the courses being offered for DoD-STD-2167A and DoD-STD-2168 should likewise be a mandatory prerequisite for any DCAS representative operating in an environment where these standards are invoked.

Software Quality Evaluation Drivers

The discipline of software quality evaluation is totally dependent on the evaluators' awareness of the software methods and measures which may be, and should be, used to form the basis for the data collection process. Without effective data collection, there will be no visibility. Without visibility, there will be no possibility for meaningful evaluation. Without meaningful evaluation, there will be no effective technical and financial management control.

Effective evaluation is a function of what is evaluated and how it is evaluated. What will be evaluated is divided between the process and the product. How it will be evaluated is a function of what can be examined or measured, the measures selected, the life cycles covered by the evaluation process, the degree of coverage and rigor of the evaluation process within each life cycle phase, and the degree to which the measurement process can be automated.

Effective evaluation also will be a function of which software development processes are automated. The more the software engineering process can be automated, the closer the industry will get to the day when defect-free software is a commonplace occurrence. The question will then be one of how much of the process is automated, and how correctly the automated functions are operating.

For example, one of the primary sources of errors in software development is poorly written specifications. The difficulties often are related to specifications which are inconsistent, incomplete, and which are not functionally validated prior to the start of the software design process.

One method for beginning to address these difficulties, in the absence of automated support tools, is to implement the inspection process at the requirements phase. This will provide some means for discovery and removal of some of the defects in the requirements. Other manual techniques such as JAD, Consensus, and The Method have been advocated. These are fundamentally a transfer of the generic concepts of the inspection process to the requirements phase.

Several requirements languages have been developed with the idea of included analysis capability, such as the PSL/PSA language developed at the University of Michigan in the early 1970s. Other languages are continuously being developed by companies and universities, such as the work done by Peter Freeman at the University of California, Irvine campus.

The way of the future will be to use automated tools for development and analysis of structured languages for requirements generation. One such application is the automated state machine-based tool ASA[1], developed in Toulouse, France, which provides software requirements generation capability, but also has a number of other critical features. The requirements are generated using IDEF data flow diagrams. The ASA tool provides particular ease in generation, modification, and manipulation of these IDEF diagrams. This was done because of the amount of time which is spent in modifying the specifications during generation.

ASA also provides the capability for automated assessment of the completeness and consistency of the specification. This can be done in real time as the specification is being created. There is no need to wait until the specification is complete to begin this verification and validation process. This analysis provides graphical output which, literally, shows where the "holes" are in the specification. The state transition matrix, for example, automatically displays a matrix showing the states and conditions of the system for each state machine component, and there should be a correspondence between these states and conditions.

Where there is not, their intersection point in the matrix is blank, and there is, therefore, a hole in the specification.

After the specification has been validated for consistency and completeness, the ASA model analysis capability may be requested to provide the measurement for hierarchical complexity of the relationship between the included functions.

Once these automated static analyses have been completed at any stage of the specification's development, the specification, or portion thereof, may be evaluated dynamically through automated rapid prototyping. In this dynamic evaluation process, the operator acts as the environment and the simulator capability of ASA acts as the system. The operator responds to menu options showing the possible actions which can be taken at that point, and the simulator builds the scenario. At any point in the creation of the scenario, the operator can query the system to find out what percent coverage of the states and transitions for each state machine component has been achieved. The operator also can query the system at any time to determine the current state of every state machine component. None of these actions in any way interferes with the scenario's continued creation.

Every state and every transition between states is examined, and in every case the analysis results indicate which states and transitions have and have not been covered 100 percent by the scenario. If there is any state or transition condition where the coverage by the prototype scenario is not 100 percent, the system is queried and automatically displays all of the possible states and transitions not covered. The operator then modifies the scenario to account for these missing conditions. Once the scenario is built, it can be archived and executed.

This process continues throughout the creation of the specification so that as the requirements are being created, they are being continuously verified and validated both statically and dynamically.

Through the use of ASA, the software developers have, therefore, before the beginning of software design, a specification which has been statically analyzed and validated for consistency, completeness and hierarchical complexity, and dynamically validated through functional rapid prototyping.

In the future, the natural extensions of such tools as this will be automated test case generation and automated design generation. Where automated design generation is done in a compilable design language, such as Ada, the programmers will no longer work at the coding level, but at the problem solving level.

Requirements for Automation

The major advancements made through the use of the inspection process were made in environments where the process was taught and applied in a highly consistent manner. The inspection process is manual, and therefore subject to a wide variety of hindrances to the most efficient and effective application of that process. Where automated tools are applied to a software development environment, the consistency is provided inherently by the automation. The important issues then become the input data on which the tool operates, and the informational content of the tool output.

This requirement for maximizing automation of the development process, including the document generation process, will be driven by the need to respond to new government standards such as DoD-STD-2167A, DoD-STD-2168, the demands for warranty in software, the need to increase productivity and quality in software developed for customer or internal use, the need to minimize the liability present with low-quality software, and the need to minimize the time programmers spend in translating requirements to design and design to code, while maximizing the time programmers spend in problem solving and analysis. It is also driven by the need to minimize the maintenance requirements for software. Maintenance in this context is referring to correction rather than enhancement (software engineering is probably the only career where adding a wing onto a building would be referred to as a maintenance task).

The necessity for maintenance is driven by two primary causes: One is faults in the code caused by human error in the code generation process, and the second is poor requirements. Both of these sources of error will have to be attacked and overcome if effective use of manpower resources is to be accomplished, and if the goals for software development in the next decade are to be reached. Our industry can no longer afford the luxury of high maintenance costs, low quality and low productivity in software development. There are too many systems being developed or conceived, such as SDI, where actual field test will be impossible or impractical. The need to know that software is correct, reliable, and maintainable (while it is being produced) will be an imperative, not a desire.

These difficulties will be overcome successfully through effective automation of as much of the software development process as possible, beginning with the requirements.

Scope of Automation

The scope of automation of software development will have to cover, as a minimum, the three major areas of:

- Management.
- Technical production of the software and associated documentation.
- Product control.

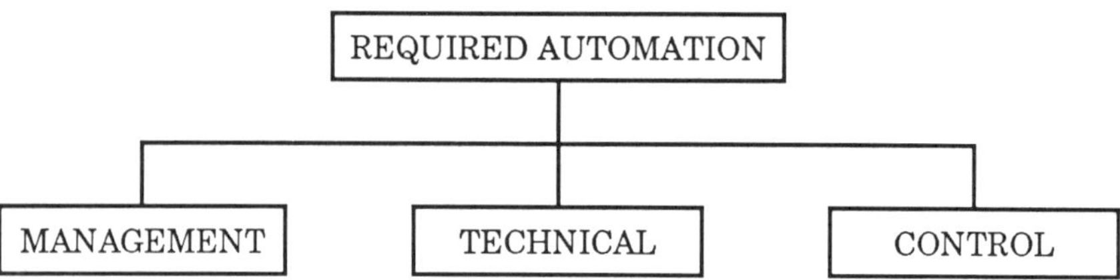

Management

In the management area, the automation required is for both planning and control. The planning information required goes far beyond normal management information system (MIS) program data where information can be stored and cross-referenced. The requirement is for software which can actually assist, in a very positive way, the planning for project control for the entire development or acquisition process.

This must be supported by other automated tools which can provide the insight, visibility, and information necessary to assist the manager in achieving true project financial and technical control from the outset, and throughout development. It should not just provide some questionably useful information when the project is half over.

The automated support required for management planning should include contingency planning, from project inception to project completion. The planning requirements include cost analysis, schedule analysis, technical assessment of the task, tradeoff analysis, manpower and skill level analysis, and risk analysis. This planning support must be integrated, and a major element in this planning process must be software quality planning.

The quality goals and requirements must be identifiable and identified. The manager must be able to examine the quality requirements and goals in terms of the project constraints such as cost, schedule and technical ability. The quality analysis will have to identify all of the individual elements of the quality requirements, including such elements as reliability, availability, and maintainability. It must also identify the quality goals, and the means to achieve those goals.

The management quality planning will then require balancing these quality requirements and goals against the project constraints. The quality plan which results will have to show how the quality requirements will be met within the constraints imposed. To balance all of these factors against each other, especially as they change during the course of a large project, will require automation. It will not be achievable through management by instinct.

Quality evaluation at the management planning level is therefore an evaluation of whether or not the quality requirements can be met under current constraints.

Management quality evaluation during production of the software is an evaluation of the current product and process quality in light of the project constraining factors. The objective of this evaluation is to optimize the quality, which means maximizing the quality within the project constraints.

Technical

The technical level will require automated means to evaluate the software in as close to a real time manner as possible, at every life cycle phase. The requirement is for a means to evaluate the software products as they are being produced so that defects which are identifiable can be avoided or eliminated immediately.

Defect elimination is the activity in place today. Defect prevention is the goal for today and the requirement for tomorrow. Defect prevention will be accomplished when the principal elements of defect introduction are eliminated. The requirements generation process must be driven away from the highly error-prone methods of the past (principally the result of writing requirements documents in prose form). Industry in general must use structured techniques such as structured requirements languages, data flow diagrams, and other requirements generation methods which lend themselves to analysis and validation. This must become an industry practice, and the government data item descriptions (DIDs) must be modified accordingly.

The software design and code generation methods must be as defect preventive as possible. This will require automation, and will mean that the programmers no longer will be generating code. They will be working at the problem solving level. Requirements generation automated tools will have to interface with automated design generation tools which produce the design from the requirements. When the automated design generation is done using a compilable design language such as Ada, then the production programmers will be doing all of their critical work at the requirements (problem solving) level. There will then be two fundamental kinds of programmers: those producing the automated tools, and those using the tools to solve application problems.

The products themselves, at every life cycle phase, must be continuously verified and validated. This will require the application of automated tools which can provide rapid evaluation of products as they are being produced so as to provide the software developers, the managers, and the customers with the information required for continual real-time assessment of progress, productivity, quality, and the information pertinent to the projected application of the product. Potential requirements changes must be assessed carefully from all viewpoints in order to avoid critical decision errors. Even an automated automobile production line has automated calipers measuring the fit of the various parts as the automobile is being assembled. The same is required for software. The automated software calipers will be needed to perform this continual assessment task. The software production process must not begin only in a defect-free condition, but must stay in a defect-free condition throughout all of the life cycle phases, including the modification phases.

Control

For the control aspects of the software development, it is necessary to control both the software and the associated documentation, and to assure that the documentation always is consistent with the code or design. Automated software documentation based on software design or code will be required to assure this consistency. Automated software configuration management tools will have to control documentation, control code, maintain software system configuration information as the software development progresses, and produce, or interface with automated producers of, the documentation or documentation changes.

The application systems being built and conceived today are much too large and complex for the industry to be satisfied with, or even to be able to rely on, manual or primitive automation to achieve effective software configuration management. Configuration management of software should begin at the initiation of the project, and continue throughout the development, operation, and modification life cycles. In the future this will be a clear requirement, and automation will be a necessity.

In such an automated environment, there will likely no longer be a need for the activities now known as PCR and FCR (Physical Configuration Review and Functional Configuration Review) for software. In a properly automated environment, these reviews will be counterproductive and wasteful of everyone's time, and money. The automated processes which will be required will be providing these functions continuously in real time.

Note

1. ASA is a copyright product of VERILOG, S. A., Toulouse, France.

CONCLUSION

The discipline of software quality evaluation is emerging and will drive and be driven by continuous introduction of automation into the software engineering process. The automated processes to be developed in the future will be based upon the lessons learned through application of manual processes, such as the inspection process. When the software engineering process has been automated in terms of: (1) requirements generation and validation, (2) design and code production, evaluation, validation and control, and (3) the documentation generation process, then the software engineering discipline shall have been industrialized. The basic tools of software industrialization already have been developed. Industrializing the software engineering process will not require a revolution. It will only require building on a fairly solid existing foundation.

When software engineering has been industrialized, it will have finally entered into the twentieth century.

APPENDIX A:

SQA MANUAL SAMPLE TABLE OF CONTENTS

SQA Procedures Manual

1.0 SQA System

1.1 SQA organization and authority

1.2 SQA tools, techniques, and methodologies

1.3 SQA procedures manual format and content description

1.4 SQA procedures review and approval cycle and authority

1.5 Applicability assessment of SQA procedures to given projects

2.0 Work tasking and authorization

2.1 Work scope definitions

2.2 Work task authorizations

2.3 SQA budgeting process

2.3.1 SQA budget management

2.3.2 SQA cost tracking

3.0 Programming standards

3.1 Requirements inspections

3.2 Design and code inspections

3.3 Programming standards inspections

3.4 Inspection data analysis

4.0 Document inspections

4.1 Inspection of contract deliverable documents

4.2 Inspection of non-deliverable documents

5.0 Configuration assurance

5.1 Library control system

5.2 Library control process inspections

5.3 Review and approval of change requests

6.0 Test verification and control

6.1 Test readiness reviews

6.2 Test monitoring

6.3 Test data records

6.4 Test data analysis

7.0 SQA inspection indicators

7.1 Bonding and validation

7.2 Stickers, labels, and seals

7.3 SQA stamps

8.0 Non-conformance and corrective action reporting

8.1 SQA audits

8.2 SQA quality assessment reports

8.3 Software trouble reports

9.0 SQA records control

9.1 SQA records control

9.2 SQA records retention

9.3 Confidentiality of SQA records

9.4 SQA inspection records data dissemination

10.0 Storage, handling, and delivery of software media

10.1 Software media handling

10.2 Software media storage

10.3 Software media shipping

11.0 Government property

11.1 Control and handling of government property

12.0 Procurement SQA

12.1 Vendor surveys

12.2 Vendor rating

12.3 Bidders conference

12.4 Vendor task and budget analysis

12.5 Post-award audits

12.6 Audit reports

12.7 Subcontractor documentation review

12.8 Subcontractor corrective action

13.0 SQA forms and instructions

APPENDIX B:

EXAMPLE OF PROPOSAL SCORING

Proposal Scoring Technique

After the technical evaluation is complete and the competitive range is determined, proposals are evaluated as follows:

a) Each offeror's cost is divided by the technical evaluation score to arrive at a "cost per point" figure.

b) Differences between offerors are determined by subtracting each offeror's score from the score of the offer with the highest technical score.

c) The "price per point" is multiplied by three times the difference between the offeror's score and the highest rated offeror to determine a cost evaluation factor.

d) The evaluation factor is added to the offeror's cost bid to arrive at an evaluated cost.

Illustration

offeror	price	technical score
A	$25,000	60
B	$40,000	95
C	$30,000	88
D	$27,000	85

offeror	price	technical score	price per point
A	$25,000	60	$416.66
B	$40,000	95	$421.05
C	$30,000	88	$340.90
D	$27,000	85	$317.65

offeror	score	difference to highest	point difference
A	60	35	105
B	95	0	0
C	88	7	21
D	85	10	30

offeror	point difference	price per point	evaluation factor
A	105	$416.66	43,749.30
B	0	$421.05	0
C	21	$340.90	7,158.90
D	30	$317.65	9,529.50

Final evaluation cost:

offeror	price	evaluation factor	evaluated cost
A	$25,000	43,749.30	$68,749.30
B	$40,000	0	$40,000.00
C	$30,000	7,158.90	$37,158.90
D	$27,000	9,529.50	$36,529.50

In this example the lowest evaluated cost would result in an award of the contract to offeror D. Note that because of the high technical score of offeror B, the two offerors which had the lower evaluated cost had to bid costs at least 25 percent lower than B in order to win the contract.

APPENDIX C:

SQA BUDGETING PROCESS FORMS

Software QA Budget Justification Sheet Input Data Internal SQA Activity: DoD-STD-2167 Program

			DoD-STD-2167 PAR NO.
1. Contract/SOW quality requirements review			
Number of contracts	0.00		
Number of SOW	2.00		
Number of hours per contract/SOW review	8.00		
hours	16.00		
Number of applicability matrices	1.00		
Applicability matrix generation	24.00		
DCAS review of matrix	8.00		
Hours	32.00		
Total hours		48.00	5.8.1.2.2 5.8
SW requirements analysis and evaluation			
Number of major functions	10.00		
Hours per major function	24.00		
Total hours		240.00	5.8.1.2.3 5.8.1.2.2.B
Requirements quality evaluation report			
Number of major functions	10.00		
Hours per function report	8.00		
Reports per function	2.00		
Total hours		160.00	5.8.1.8 5.8.1.9
2. SW quality evaluation plan			5.8.2.1
Initial plan generation (hrs.)	80.00		5.8.2.2
Contract months	36.00		5.8.2.3

Estimated number of revisions (quarterly)	11.00		
Hours per revision	40.00		
DCAS review/evaluation per plan	24.00		
DCAS comment incorporation per plan (hrs.)	16.00		
Total hours		1,000.00	5.8.1.1 5.8.1.2.2.B
3. Evaluation requirements education			5.8.1.7
Number of hours per class	4.00		
Number of classes	1.00		
Total hours		4.00	5.8.1.1
4. Design inspection data analysis			
Number of hours per module	1.25		
Number of design modules	45.00		
Modules are estimated as estimated SLOC divided by 100			
Total hours		56.00	5.8.1.2.4 5.8.1.2.5
Design inspection data entry: number of weeks	20.00		5.8.1.2
Number of hours per week	0.50		
Total hours		10.00	5.8.1.2.4 5.8.1.2.5
5. Code inspection data analysis			
Number of hours per module	1.25		
Number of code modules	45.00		
Modules are estimated as estimated SLOC divided by 100			
Total hours		56.25	5.8.1.2.6 5.8.1.2
Code inspection data entry: number of weeks	15.00		
Number of hours per week	0.50		
Total hours		7.50	5.8.1.2.6
Inspection evaluation reports			

Inspection reports			
Reports per month	1.00		
Hours per report	8.00		
Number of months in design and code	24.00		5.8.1.2.2.B
Total hours		192.00	5.8.1.8
			5.8.1.9
			5.8.2.1
6. SW CM spec. tree review			5.8.2.2
Operational SW	1.00		5.8.1.2
One-time review			
Total hours		4.00	5.8.1.2.2.A
			5.8.2.1
			5.8.1.8
7. SW CM spec. tree review			
Diagnostics SW	1.00		
One-time review			
Total hours		4.00	5.8.1.2.2.A
			5.8.2.1
			5.8.1.8
8. SW CM spec. tree review			
Firmware	1.00		
One-time review			
Total hours		4.00	5.8.1.2.2.A
			5.8.2.1
			5.8.1.8
9. SW deliverable documentation review			
Number of hours per document	16.00		
Number of documents to review (prelim)	10.00		
Number of documents to review (final)	10.00		
Total hours		320.00	5.8.1.2.1
			5.8.1.8
10. Attend/participate in PDR			5.8.1.2
Number of PDRs	1.00		5.8.1.2.2.B
Number of days for PDR	2.00		5.8.1.7
Total hours		16.00	5.8.1.2.4
11. Attend/participate in CDR			
Number of CDRs	1.00		
Number of days for CDR	2.00		
Total hours		16.00	5.8.1.2.5

12. Quality evaluation audits of SW development performed quarterly			
Number of hours per audit	16.00		
Number of audits	12.00		
Hours	192.00		
Audit reports			
Hours per audit report	4.00		
Number of audits	12.00		
Hours	48.00		
Total hours		240.00	5.8.1.3
			5.8.1.8
13. Quality evaluation audits of			
diagnostics development			5.8.1.9
performed quarterly			5.8.1.2
Number of hours per audit	8.00		5.8.1.2.2.B
Number of audits	12.00		5.8.2.1
Hours	96.00		
Audit reports			
Hours per audit report	4.00		
Number of audits	12.00		
Hours	48.00		
Total hours		144.00	5.8.1.3
			5.8.1.8
14. Quality evaluation audits of			
firmware development			5.8.1.9
performed quarterly			5.8.1.2
Number of hours per audit	8.00		5.8.1.2.2.B
Number of audits	12.00		5.8.2.1
Hours	96.00		
Audit reports			
Hours per audit report	4.00		
Number of audits	12.00		
Hours	48.00		
Total hours		144.00	5.8.1.3
			5.8.1.8
15. Quality evaluation audits of			
T&I SW control			5.8.1.9
performed quarterly			5.8.1.2
Number of hours per audit	8.00		5.8.1.2.2.B
Number of audits	12.00		5.8.2.1

Hours	96.00		
Audit reports			
Hours per audit report	4.00		
Number of audits	12.00		
Hours	48.00		
Total hours		144.00	5.8.1.3
16. Quality evaluation audits of SW CM			5.8.1.2
Performed quarterly			5.8.1.2.2.B
Number of hours per audit	8.00		5.8.2.1
Number of audits	12.00		
Hours	96.00		
Audit reports			
Hours per audit report	4.00		
Number of audits	12.00		
Hours	48.00		
Total hours		144.00	5.8.1.3
			5.8.1.8
17. Customer interface (including DCAS)			5.8.1.9
Twice monthly meetings			5.8.1.2
Hours per meeting	0.25		5.8.1.2.2.B
Hours per month	0.50		5.8.2.1
Number of contract months	36.00		
Hours		18.00	5.8.1.4
			5.8.2.2
Support DCAS SQA program evaluation			
Quarterly			
Hours per SQA PE	2.00		
Number of quarters	12.00		
Total hours		24.00	5.8.1.4
			5.8.2.2
Support DCAS SW development PE			
Quarterly			
Hours per SQA PE	2.00		
Number of quarters	12.00		
Total hours		24.00	5.8.1.4
			5.8.2.2
Support DCAS SW CM PE			
Quarterly			
Hours per SQA PE	2.00		

Number of quarters	12.00		
Total hours		24.00	5.8.1.4
			5.8.2.2
Support DCAS SW test PE			
Quarterly			
Hours per SQA PE	2.00		
Number of quarters	12.00		
Total hours		24.00	5.8.1.4
			5.8.2.2
18. Regular meetings (status, etc.)			
Number of meetings per month	4.00		
Hours per meeting	1.50		
Hours per month	6.00		
Number of contract months	36.00		
Total hours		216.00	5.8.2.2
19. Program office interface			
Hours per month	10.00		
Number of contract months	36.00		
Total hours		360.00	5.8.2.2
20. Test monitor			
Hours per week	3.00		
Number of weeks of test	48.00		
Total hours		144.00	5.8.1.2.6
			5.8.1.2.7
Test readiness inspection			5.8.1.2.8
One inspection per acceptance test			5.8.1.2.2.B
Hours per test readiness inspection	8.00		5.8.2.1
Number of acceptance tests	1.00		
Total hours		8.00	5.8.1.2.6
			5.8.1.2.7
21. Test witness			5.8.1.2.8
Number of acceptance tests	1.00		5.8.1.4
Number of days per acceptance test	1.50		
Total hours		12.00	5.8.1.2.6
			5.8.1.2.7
22. PTR review			5.8.1.2.8
Hours per week	1.00		5.8.1.2.2.B
Number of weeks of test	48.00		
Total hours		48.00	5.8.1.10

23. PTR data analysis			
Hours per week	3.00		
Number of weeks of test	48.00		
Total hours		144.00	5.8.1.10
			5.8.1.2.2.B
PTR evaluation reports			5.8.2.1
PTR analysis report			
Reports per month	1.00		
Hours per report	8.00		
Number of months in test	12.00		
Total hours		96.00	5.8.1.10
			5.8.1.9
24. SW media handling (tapes, etc.)			5.8.1.2.2.B
Number of builds	20.00		
Number of hours per build	0.50		
Total hours		10.00	5.8.1.4
			5.8.1.2.2.B
25. SW delivery processing (shipping)			
Hours per shipment	2.00		
Number of shipments	2.00		
Total hours		4.00	5.8.1.4
			5.8.1.2.2.B
26. Subcontractor SW receipt processing			
Hours per delivery to our company	1.50		
Number of deliveries (including formal deliveries and informal drops)	0.00		
Total hours		0.00	5.8.1.6
			5.8.1.2.2.B
27. SCCB activity			
Hours per build	1.00		
Number of builds	20.00		
Total hours		20.00	5.8.1.2.8
			5.8.1.2.2.B
28. Engineering notice processing			5.8.2.1
Number of final releases:			

Operational SW	1.00		
Diagnostics SW	1.00		
Firmware/microcode	1.00		
Number of hours per release	2.00		
Total hours		6.00	5.8.1.2.8 5.8.1.2.2.B
29. Software physical configuration audit support			
One PCA preparation period	8.00		
One actual software PCA (full-time first day; on call rest of time)	8.00		
One PCA per delivered product			
Number of PCAs	1.00		
Total hours		16.00	5.8.1.4
PCA discrepancy resolution			
Average hours per PCA	16.00		
Number of PCAs	1.00		
Total hours		16.00	5.8.1.4
30. Installation and checkout			
Installation and checkout required?	1.00		
Number of modules	45.00		
Evaluation hours per module	1.50		
Total hours		68.00	5.8.1.5
31. Quality cost data analysis			
Data collection:			
Number of modules	45.00		
Number of documents	20.00		
From SW development (hrs.)	2.25		
From SW test (hrs.)	67.50		
From SW engineering (hrs.)	1.13		
From SW configuration management (hrs.)	5.00		
From SW quality assurance (hrs.)	32.50		
Data analysis and documentation:			
Number of reports: quarterly	12.00		
Hours per report	24.00		
Total hours		396.00	5.8.1.11 5.8.2.1

32. Software line item certification			
Number of line items	90.00		
Data collection/reporting per item (hrs.)	16.00		
Total hours		1,440.00	5.8.2.3 5.8.1.2.2.B
33. Management (10 percent)		607.00	5.8.2.1 5.8.1.7
Total budget hours (round to nearest hour)		6,679	

Budget and work task description

Task title: software quality assurance

WBS/work package number:

Total hours: 6,679

Product of subtask (reports, etc.):

SQA quality evaluation reports

SQA product certification reports

SQA quality evaluation plan(s)

Description of subtask	Subtask hours (by labor code) A	B	C	D
1. Contract/SOW quality review	0	448	0	0
2. SW quality evaluation plan	0	1,000	0	0
3. Evaluation requirements education	0	4	0	0
4. Design inspection data analysis	0	56	10	0
5. Code inspection data analysis plus walk-through RE	0	248	8	0
6. SW CM spec. tree review, operations	0	4	0	0
7. SW CM spec. tree review, diagnostics	0	4	0	0
8. SW CM spec. tree review, firmware	0	4	0	0
9. Software deliverable documentation review	0	320	0	0
10. Attend/participate in PDR	0	16	0	0
11. Attend/participate in CDR	0	16	0	0

12.	Quality evaluation audits of SW development	0	240	0	0
13.	Quality evaluation audits of diagnostics development	0	144	0	0
14.	Quality evaluation audits of firmware development	0	144	0	0
15.	Quality evaluation audits of T&I SW control	0	144	0	0
16.	Quality evaluation audits of SW configuration mgmt.	0	144	0	0
17.	Customer interface (including DCAS)	0	114	0	0
18.	Regular meetings (weekly status, etc.)	0	216	0	0
19.	Program office interface	0	360	0	0
20.	Test monitor	0	152	0	0
21.	Test witness	0	12	0	0
22.	PTR review	0	0	48	0
23.	PTR data analysis and evaluation reports	0	240	0	0
24.	SW media handling (tapes, etc.)	0	0	10	0
25.	SW delivery (shipment) processing	0	0	4	0
26.	SW receipt (from sub. or customer)	0	0	0	0
27.	SCCB activity	0	20	0	0
28.	EN processing	0	0	6	0
29.	Software PCA support	0	32	0	0
30.	Installation and checkout	0	68	0	0
31.	Quality cost data collection/analysis	0	396	0	0
32.	SW line item certification	0	1,440	0	0
33.	Management (10 percent)	607			
					Totals
		607	5,986	86	0
	Avg/mo:	17	166	2	0
	Number cont mo	36			

Basis for estimate:
Determined by subdividing task per scope of work as outlined in proposal ground rules. Effort involved in each sub-task is based on experience.

Time period: Date:
Originator: Approvals:
Reference: DoD-STD-2167, Paragraph 5.8.1.6
Budget justification sheet input data
Software Procurement QA (per subcontractor)

1. Contract/SOW quality review		
Number of contracts	1.00	
Number of SOW	1.00	
Number of hours per contract/SOW	8.00	
Hours	16.00	
Vendor software survey	16.00	
Survey travel days	2.00	
Hours	32.00	
Review sub. applicability matrix	1.00	
Applicability matrix review	24.00	
Hours	24.00	
Total hours		72.00
2. Review sub. SW quality evaluation plan		
New plan	1.00	
Number of planned revisions	11.00	
Hours per new plan	24.00	
Hours per revised plan	16.00	
Total hours		200.00
3. SW quality evaluation orientation for sub.		
Number of hours per orientation	8.00	
Number of orientation sessions	1.00	
Total hours		8.00
4. Design inspection data analysis		
Number of hours per module	1.25	
Number of modules	45.00	
Modules are estimated as estimated SLOC divided by 100		
Total hours		56.25
Inspection data entry: number of weeks	20.00	
Number of hours per week	0.50	
Total hours		10.00
5. Code inspection data analysis		
Number of hours per module	1.25	
Number of modules	45.00	
Modules are estimated as estimated SLOC divided by 100		
Total hours		56.25
Code inspection data entry: number of WEE	15.00	

Number hours per week	0.50	
Total hours		7.50
6. SW CM spec. tree review		
Operational SW	1.00	
One-time review		
Total hours		4.00
7. SW CM spec. tree review		
Diagnostics SW	1.00	
One-time review		
Total hours		4.00
8. SW CM spec. tree review	1.00	
Firmware		
One-time review		
Total hours		4.00
9. SW subcontractor documentation review		
Number of hours per document	8.00	
Number of documents to review (prelim.)	10.00	
Number of documents to review (final)	10.00	
Total hours		160.00
10. Attend/participate in PDR		
Number of PDRs	1.00	
Number of days for PDR	2.00	
Number of travel days	2.00	
Total hours		32.00
11. Attend/participate in CDR		
Number of CDRs	1.00	
Number of days for CDR	2.00	
Number of travel days	2.00	
Total hours		32.00
12. Audits of SW development		
Quarterly: number of subcontract months	36.00	
Number of hours per audit	8.00	
Number of audits	12.00	
Number of travel days	2.00	
Total hours		288.00
Audit reports		
Hours per audit report	8.00	

Number of audits	12.00	
Hours	96.00	
Total hours		384.00
13. Audits of subcont. diagnostics development		
Performed quarterly: number of contract months	36.00	
Number of hours per audit	8.00	
Number of audits	12.00	
Hours	96.00	
(Travel hrs. included in item 12)		
Audit reports		
Hours per audit report	4.00	
Number of audits	12.00	
Hours	48.00	
Total hours		144.00
14. Audits of firmware development		
Quarterly: number of contract months	36.00	
Number of hours per audit	8.00	
Number of audits	12.00	
Hours	96.00	
(Travel hrs. included in item 12)		
Audit reports		
Hours per audit report	4.00	
Number of audits	12.00	
Hours	48.00	
Total hours		144.00
15. Audits of sub SQA		
Quarterly: number of contract months	36.00	
Number of hours per audit	8.00	
Number of audits	12.00	
Hours	96.00	
(Travel hrs. included in item 12)		
Audit reports		
Hours per audit report	4.00	
Number of audits	12.00	
Hours	48.00	
Total hours		144.00
16. Audits of SW CM		
Quarterly: number of contract months	36.00	
Number of hours per audit	8.00	
Number of audits	12.00	

Hours	96.00	
(Travel hrs. included in item 12)		
Audit reports		
Hours per audit report	4.00	
Number of audits	12.00	
Hours	48.00	
Total hours		144.00
17. Customer interface (incl. DCAS)		
Twice monthly meetings		
Hours per meeting	1.00	
Hours per month	2.00	
Number of months	36.00	
Total hours		72.00
Support DCAS SQA PE		
Quarterly		
Hours per SQA PE	2.00	
Number of quarters	12.00	
Total hours		24.00
18. Program review meetings at sub.		
Number of meetings per month	1.00	
Hours per meeting	16.00	
Hours per month	16.00	
Number of months	36.00	
Number of travel days per meeting	2.00	
Total hours		1,152.00
19. Program office interface		
Hours per month	5.00	
Number of months	36.00	
Total hours		180.00
20. Test monitor at subcontractor		
Hours per month	3.00	
Number of months of test	48.00	
Total hours		144.00
Test readiness inspection		
One inspection per acceptance test		
Hours per test readiness inspection	8.00	
Number of acceptance tests	1.00	
Total hours		8.00
21. Test witness of sub. acceptance test		
Number of acceptance tests	1.00	

Number of days per acceptance test	2.00	
Travel days per test	2.00	
Total hours		32.00
22. Review of subcontractor PTR report		
Hours per weeks	1.00	
Number of weeks of test	48.00	
Total hours		48.00
23. Subcontractor PTR data analysis		
Hours per week	3.00	
Number of weeks of test	48.00	
Total hours		144.00
24. SW media handling (tapes, etc.)		
Number of deliveries to sub.	20.00	
Number hours per delivery	0.50	
Total hours		10.00
25. Delivered SW master library control		
Hours per shipment	2.00	
Number of shipments	2.00	
Total hours		4.00
26. Subcontractor SW receipt processing		
Hours per delivery to prime contractor	1.50	
Number of deliveries (incl. formal deliveries and informal drops)	0.00	
Total hours		0.00
27. SCCB activity		
Hours per build at prime cont.	1.00	
Number of builds	20.00	
Total hours		20.00
28. EN processing		
Number of final releases:		
Operational SW	1.00	
Diagnostics SW	1.00	
Firmware/microcode	1.00	
Number of hours per release	2.00	
Total hours		6.00
29. SQA data reports (production and distribution)		
Inspection reports: subcontractor data		
Reports per month	1.00	
Hours per report	8.00	

Number of months in design and code	24.00	
Total hours		192.00
PTR analysis report		
Reports per month	1.00	
Hours per report	8.00	
Number of months in test	12.00	
Total hours		96.00
30. Software PCA support		
One PCA preparation period	8.00	
One actual software PCA (Full-time first day; on call rest of time)	8.00	
One PCA per delivered product		
Number of PCAs	1.00	
Total hours		16.00
PCA discrepancy resolution		
Average hours per PCA	16.00	
Number of PCAs	1.00	
Travel days per PCA	2.00	
Total hours		48.00
31. Management (10 percent)		379.00
Total budget hours (round to nearest hour)		4,165

Budget and work task description
Work task: software quality assurance
Subtask: software procurement quality assurance
WBS/work package number:
Total hours: 4,147
Product of subtask: (reports, etc.)
SQA data reports
SQA product inspection reports
Subcontractor audit reports

	Subtask hours (by labor code)			
Description of subtask	**A**	**B**	**C**	**D**
1. Contract/SOW quality review	0	72	0	0
2. SQA plan review	0	200	0	0
3. Design/code inspection class	8	0	0	0
4. Design insp. data analysis	0	56	10	0
5. Code insp. data analysis	0	56	8	0

6.	SW CM spec. tree review (operations)	0	4	0	0
7.	SW CM spec. tree review (diagnostics)	0	4	0	0
8.	SW CM spec. tree review (firmware)	0	4	0	0
9.	Software documentation review	0	160	0	0
10.	Attend/participate in PDR	0	32	0	0
11.	Attend/participate in CDR	0	32	0	0
12.	Audits of SW development	0	384	0	0
13.	Audits of sub. diagnostics development	0	144	0	0
14.	Audits of firmware development	0	144	0	0
15.	Audits of subcontractor SQA	0	144	0	0
16.	Audits of SW configuration mgmt.	0	144	0	0
17.	Customer interface (incl. DCAS)	0	96	0	0
18.	Program review meetings at sub.	0	1,152	0	0
19.	Program office interface	0	180	0	0
20.	Test monitor	0	152	0	0
21.	Test witness	0	32	0	0
22.	PTR review	0	0	48	0
23.	PTR data analysis	0	144	0	0
24.	SW media handling (tapes, etc.)	0	0	10	0
25.	Delivered SW master library control	0	0	4	0
26.	SW receipt (from sub. or customer)	0	0	0	0
27.	SCCB activity	0	20	0	0
28.	EN processing	0	0	6	0
29.	SQA data reports (production and distribution	0	288	0	0
30.	PCA support and action item resolution	0	48	0	
31.	Management (10 percent)	379			
			Totals		
		385	3,676	86	0
	Average hours per month (rounded)	11	102	2	0
	Number of months:	36			

APPENDIX D:

EXAMPLE OF AN APPLICABILITY MATRIX FORMAT

Applicability Matrix Format

Format is a cross-reference between the governing documents, and the provisions of the QA plan, SQA procedures, internal procedures, and any required special procedures.

document	paragraph number	QA plan paragraph	SQA proc. number	internal proc. no.	special proc.
MIL-Q-9858A	1.5.2	2.3	1.2.3	C.1.2.3	N/A
	*	*	*	*	*
	*	*	*	*	*
	*	*	*	*	*
DoD-STD-2167	2.5.6	3.5.4	2.5.7	N/A	N/A
	3.6.8	6.7.4	—	—	7.5.9
	*	*	*	*	*
	*	*	*	*	*
	*	*	*	*	*

APPENDIX E:

EXAMPLES OF SQA AUDIT CHECKLISTS

Software Quality Assurance Audit Checklist

Date:

Company:

Contact:

Auditor:

Location:

Participants: ______________________________

____

____

****
Note: Numbers in parentheses refer to paragraph numbers in MIL-STD-1679 or MIL-S-52779A.
****

1. Types of software to be delivered:

   (1679-3.2.1) operational ______

   (1679-3.2.2) PM/FL ______

   (1679-3.2.3) trainer ______

   (1679-3.2.4) support ______

   (1679-1.2;3.2) firmware ______

2. Is there a quality assurance organization? ____ Does this organization perform software quality assurance?____ (1679-5.9; 5.9.1); (52779A-1.2)

3. Is the organization independent of those whom the organization monitors? ____ (1679-5.9.1.1)

4. Has SQA planned, developed, and implemented an SQA program, including practices and procedures to assure compliance with all software requirements of the contract? (52779A-3.1)

5. Is documented contract SQA plan in place? (1679-6.1m); (52779A-3.1)

6. Is this contractor SQA plan generated by subcontractor (Y N) ____ , or was the prime contractor SQA plan adopted for this contract (Y N) ____ ?

7. Is there a written set of SQA procedures in place governing the internal SQA activity to be performed? (1679-4.4; 5.9); (52779A-3.1)

8. Do these procedures enable SQA to assure that all of the requirements of MIL-STD-1679 are followed:

   a. Applied to operational, PM/FL, trainer, support software? ____ (1679-3.2.1-3.2.4)

   b. Design exactly implements PPS? ____ (1679-4.2)

   c. Use only HOL, unless waiver granted? ____ (1679-4.3; 5.5.3)

   d. Software CM program established? ____ (1679-4.5)

   e. Subcontractor quality control? ____ (1679-4.6); (52779A-3.3)

9. Does the SQA program adequately address:

   a. SQA tools, techniques, and methods? ____ (52779A-3.2.1)

   b. Review/evaluation of software design? ____ (52779A-3.2.2)

   c. Work certification? ____ (52779A-3.2.3)

   d. Documentation standards and practices? ____ (52779A-3.2.4)

e. Computer program library controls? ____ (52779A-3.2.5)

f. Procedures for reviews and audits? ____ (52779A-3.2.6)

g. The SQA/CM relationship? ____ (52779A-3.2.7)

h. Procedures for assuring the integrity of software products during preparation for delivery? ____ (52779A–5.0)

i. Application of SQA to firmware? ____ (1679-1.2)

10. Does SQA review the PPS for conformance to the DID requirements? _____ Does SQA assure that the PPS is adequately reviewed prior to implementation? ____ (1679-5.1.2; 5.9.1.4; 5.12.3.3)

    Is there objective evidence of such review on file ____ ?

11. Is there a similar review of the PDS? ____ (1679-5.2.2.1; 5.12.3.3)

    Is there objective evidence of such review on file?____

12. Is there a similar review of the IDS? ____ (1679-5.2.3; 5.12.3.3)

    Is there objective evidence of such review on file? ____

13. Does SQA assure that the system resources are determined and do not exceed the allowed limits? ____ (1679-5.1.3; 5.2.2.4; 5.5.2; 5.10.1) (Tadstand D)

14. Does SQA assure that the software is developed in a top-down structured manner? ____ (1679-5.2; 5.5)

    Is there objective evidence on file?____

15. Does SQA assure that the proposed program architecture is verified as to its capacity to support the computational load imposed by maximum operation of all functions? ____ (1679-5.2)

Is there objective evidence on file?____

16. Have any constraints of the language used or of the support software been defined? ____ (1679-5.2.2.5)

    Is there objective evidence on file?____

17. Have coding standards and conventions been established? ____ Are they in conformance with Section 5.3 of MIL-STD-1679 as to:

    Control structures (1679-5.3.1) ____________________

    Include/copy segments (1679-5.3.2) ____________________

    Entry-exit structure (1679-5.3.3) ____________________

    Program traceability (1679-5.3.4) ____________________

    Self-modification (1679-5.3.5) ____________________

    Recursive programs (1679-5.3.6) ____________________

    Size (1679-5.3.7) ____________________

    Branching (1679-5.3.8) ____________________

    How has this been verified? ____________________

    ____

18. Have the coding conventions of Section 5.4 of MIL-STD-1679 been established, including the requirements for a prologue? ____ (1679-5.4; 5.4.4.1; 5.4.4.2)

    How has this been verified? ____________________

    ____

19. Does SQA assure that a code walk-through or inspection is conducted for each software module? ____ (1679-5.5)

    Is there objective evidence on file?____

20. Does SQA conduct quality audits throughout the software development phases, beginning with design? ____ (1679-5.9.1.2); (52779A-3.2.6)

    Is there objective evidence of the audits on file?____

    Which functions are audited? ______________________________

    ____

    Is there an audit schedule on file? ____ (52779A-3.2.6)

21. Does SQA participate in design walk-throughs? ____ (1679-5.9.1.3)

    In what way? ______________________________________

    ____

22. Does SQA assure contractual correctness of all deliverable items? ____ (1679-5.9.1.7)

    How has this been verified? ___________________________

    ____

23. Does SQA witness any tests? ____ (1679-5.9.1.6)

    If so, to what extent and at what levels? _______________

    ____

    ____

    Is there objective evidence on file? ____

24. Are there SQA procedures to assure that software requirements are analyzed to determine testability? ____ (52779A-3.2.8a)

25. Are there SQA procedures to assure that the test requirements and criteria are reviewed for adequacy, feasibility, traceability, and satisfaction of requirements? ____ (52779A-3.2.8b)

26. Are there SQA procedures for review of test documentation for compliance with contractual requirements? ____ (52779A-3.2.8c)

27. Are there SQA procedures to verify that testing is conducted in accordance with approved plans and procedures? ____ (52779A-3.2.8d)

28. Are there SQA procedures to certify that the test results are the actual findings of the test? ____ (52779A-3.2.8e)

29. Are there SQA procedures for the review and certification of test reports? ____ (52779A-3.2.8f)

30. Are there SQA procedures to ensure that the test-related materials are maintained? ____ (52779A-3.2.8g)

31. Are there SQA procedures to ensure that support software, used to develop and test software, is acceptable to the customer? ____ (52779A-3.2.8h)

32. Is there a software trouble reporting system in place? ____ (52779A-3.2.9 through 3.2.9e)

    Does it meet the intent of MIL-STD-1679 paragraph 5.8.5?____

    Does it prioritize errors according to paragraph 5.8.5.2?

33. Is there a patch control system? ____ (1679-5.5.4; 5.10.3.2)

    How has this been verified? ____________________

    ____

Configuration management/control

34. Does the SQA program specify the relationship between the SQA program and the software CM program? ____ (52779A-3.2.7)

    ____

    ____

35. Are there documented procedures for assuring that the objectives of the software CM program are being attained? ____ (52779A-3.2.7)

    ____

    ____

36. Is there a procedure for producing, updating, and controlling source and object libraries of the software under development? ____ (1679-5.5.4); (52779A-3.2.5)

37. Is software maintained in both source and object form? ____ (1679-5.5.4)

    How has this been verified?______________________

    ____

38. Is there protection against unauthorized modification of the libraries? ____ (52779A-3.2.5; 3.2.8c)

    How has this been verified? ______________________

    ____

39. Is there a cross-reference listing maintained? ____ (1679-5.5.6.2)

    How has this been verified? ______________________

    ____

40. Is a system load map maintained? ____(1679-5.5.7)

    How has this been verified? ______________________

    ____

41. Have system baselines been established? ____ (1679-5.11.1.1)

    How has this been verified? ______________________

    ____

42. Is there a procedure for control and baseline of all firmware up to the point of burn-in? ____ (1679-1.2; 3.2)

43. Has a proper document identification system been established? (1679-5.11.1.2)

    How has this been verified? ______________________

    ____

44. Have written procedures been established for formal control of all documents, program materials, and the development support library? ____ (1679-5.11.2)

    How has this been verified? ______________________

    ____

45. Is there an SCCB in operation? ____ Is SQA a participant on the SCCB? ____ (1679-5.11.2.1; 5.11.2.3)

    Does the SCCB have written procedures? ____What software is controlled by the SCCB? ______________________

    ____

    ____

    How has this been verified? ______________________

    ____

46. Is there documentation describing any SQA procedures for resolution of process or product problems/issues identified in any SQA audits or reviews, including response obligations of the audited or reviewed function? ____

    Is there objective evidence of the resolution activity in the SQA file? ____

47. Does either SQA or SWCM assure that there is a completely accurate correlation between the implemented code and the descriptive documentation for that code? (1679-4.5)

    ____

Additional comments:

Documents received:

Action items:

number	action	assignee

MIL-S-52779A Requirements Software Quality Assurance Program Requirements

Paragraph/requirement

1.2: Establish SQA program. Implement the SQA program. Purpose of the program is to assure that all software developed, *acquired*, or otherwise provided under the contract complies with the requirements of the contract.

1.3: The contractor is responsible for compliance with *all* provisions of the contract and for furnishing software which complies with all of the requirements of the contract.

3.1: The contractor shall plan, develop, and implement an SQA program which includes *practices and procedures to assure compliance with all software requirements of the contract.* The SQA program shall be part of the management reporting system throughout the life of the contract.

The program shall provide for the detection, reporting, analysis, and correction of software problems and deficiencies. Contract quality assurance personnel shall have the responsibility, authority, and organizational freedom to evaluate software activities, identify problems, and initiate or recommend corrective action.

3.2.2: The quality assurance plan shall reference or document the procedures by which design documentation is reviewed to evaluate design logic, fulfillment of requirements, completeness, *and compliance with specified standards.*

3.2.4: The quality assurance plan shall reference or document the procedures to be applied to assure that software documentation complies with the standards, practices and conventions, and delivery of correct documentation and change information to the customer.

3.2.6: The quality assurance plan shall reference or document the procedures for preparation and execution of audits and reviews and for establishing the traceability of the initial contract requirements through the successive baselines, and for ensuring that reviews and audits are conducted in accordance with the prescribed procedures. The audit and review schedule shall be referenced or stated in the plan.

3.2.7: The plan shall specify the relationship between SQA and software CM and shall reference or document the procedures for assuring that the objectives of the CM program are being attained.

5.0: The plan shall reference or document the procedures for assuring the integrity of software products during handling, storage, preservation, packaging, and shipping.

MIL-Q-9858A Requirements Quality Program Requirements

Paragraph/requirement

1.2: Requires the establishment of a quality program to assure the compliance with contract requirements.

1.3: The quality program shall assure adequate quality throughout *all* areas of contract performance.

All supplies and services shall be controlled at all points necessary to assure conformance to contractual requirements.

The program shall provide for prevention and ready detection of discrepancies and for timely and positive corrective action. The contractor shall make objective evidence of quality conformance readily available to the customer.

The program shall include an effective control of purchased products and subcontracted work.

1.4: The quality program requirements set forth in this specification shall be satisfied in addition to all detail requirements contained in the SOW or contract.

3.1: Quality assurance personnel shall have sufficient, well-defined responsibility, authority, and freedom to identify and evaluate quality problems and to initiate, recommend or provide solutions.

Management shall regularly review the status and adequacy of the quality program.

3.3: The quality program shall assure that all work affecting quality shall be prescribed in clear and complete documented instructions appropriate to the circumstances and compatible with acceptance criteria of that work effort. Preparation of and compliance with work instructions shall be monitored as a function of the quality program.

3.4: The contractor shall maintain and use any records or data essential to the economical *and effective* operation of the quality program. These records shall be available for review by the customer and copies of individual records shall be furnished the customer on request.

The quality program shall assure that records are complete and reliable. The quality program shall provide for the analysis and use of records as a basis for management action.

3.5: The quality program shall detect promptly and correct assignable conditions adverse to quality. Corrective action will extend to the performance of all suppliers and vendors, and will be responsive to data and product forwarded from users.

4.1: The quality program must provide complete coverage of all information necessary to produce an article in complete conformity with requirements of the design.

5.1: The contractor is responsible for assuring that all supplies and services procured from suppliers conform to the contract requirements.

The contractor shall utilize, to the fullest extent, objective evidence of quality furnished by his suppliers.

6.2: Criteria for approval or rejection shall be provided for all inspection of product and monitoring of methods, equipment and personnel. Means for identifying approved and rejected product shall be provided.

6.3: The quality program shall assure that there is a system for final inspection and test of completed products.

6.7: The contractor shall maintain a positive system for identifying the inspection status of products.

Software Quality Assurance (SQA) Audit Form

Header

Date:	
Subcontractor:	Location:
Contact person:	Phone:
Contract:	SDRL ref.:
Subsystem:	Program ID:

Participants: ____

____

Part I
(What is to be covered)

SQA procedures manual reference specification: MIL-S-52779(A)

Manual content	**Minimal acceptable coverage**
Paragraph no.	**Item description**
3.2.1	organizational responsibilities
3.2.2	design documentation—PPS, PDS, . . .
3.2.3	work product cost reporting (work certification)
3.2.4	compliance matrices
3.2.5	library controls
3.2.6	reviews and audits
3.2.7	configuration management
3.2.8	test readiness testing
3.2.9	corrective action
3.3	subcontractor control
5.0	preparation for delivery—integrity

Software Quality Assurance (SQA) Audit Form

Header

Date:
Subcontractor: Location:
Contact person: Phone:
Contract: SDRL ref.:
Subsystem: Program ID:

Participants: ______________________________

____

Part II
(How are the procedures carried out)

Reference standard: MIL-STD-1679
Objective evidence for each item to verify implementation

Paragraph no.	Question	Objective evidence reference
	1) Deliverable software/documentation	
3.2.1	operational ______________	______
3.2.2	PM/FL ______________	______
3.2.3	trainer ______________	______
3.2.4	support ______________	______
1.2; 3.2	firmware (microcode) ____	______
5.9.1	2) A software quality assurance organization which has corporate reporting responsibilities independent of the software development and engineering groups is in place	

____

Paragraph no.	Question	Objective evidence reference
5.9; 4.4	2A) Work instructions (procedures) are documented and implemented as per the quality assurance plan	________
5.9	3) There is a requirement for a software quality plan	________
	Plan is complete and approved	________
5.9	4) A government procurement agency or authorized representative has reviewed the SQA procedures (info only)	________
5.1; 5.2	5) Is there a requirement for a PPS? ____ PDS? ____	
	There is objective evidence that the method used by SQA to ensure that the PPS accurately reflects the software product performance requirements of the contract.	______

Paragraph no.	Question	Objective evidence reference
5.3	6) Coding standards have been established and are in conformance with Section 5.3 of MIL-STD-1679 as to:	
	control structures ________	
	include/copy segments ______	
	entry/exit structure ________	
	program traceability _______	
	self-modification __________	
	recursive programs ________	
	size ____________________	
	branching ________________	
5.4	7) The following coding conventions have been established and implemented:	
	prologue requirements __________	
	symbolic parameterization _______	
	numeric conventions ____________	
	uniform naming convention ______	
5.5; 5.9	8) During the software production process the following items are implemented:	
	top-down development _______	
	resource management _______	
	HOL or waiver granted ______	
	library control system _______	
	patch control system ________	
	patch logs __________________	
	listings:	
	source ____________________	

Paragraph no.	Question	Objective evidence reference
	cross-reference ______ load maps ______ design inspections ______ code inspections ______	
5.6	9) All deliverable software is capable of being regenerated by IBM support software or required contractual-delivered support software ______	
5.7	10) There is a contractual requirement to deliver an operator and/or user manual(s) ______	
5.8	11) There is an SDRL requirement for a: software test plan ______ test specification ______ test procedure ______ test report ______ The test plan covers the following: performance (HW and SW integration) ______ subprogram (process/string) ______ module/unit ______ SQA signs off on adequacy of test report ______	

Paragraph no.	Question	Objective evidence reference
	Each test has test procedures and reports	
	______	
	SQA monitors and signs off on test procedures and completed test reports	
	______	
	SQA escalates unresolved test problems to upper management	
	______	
	There are SQA procedures that assure acceptance test materials are maintained (i.e., as run test procedures, controlled software, test log, environment tapes, computer system outputs)	

Paragraph no.	Question	Compliance forms reference
5.11	12) All deliverable development software has a baseline part number identification to the following level:	
	system ______________________	
	subsystem (major function) ______	
	program ______________________	
	module ______________________	
	Do you have a software configuration control board (SCCB)?	
	______	

Paragraph no.	Question	Compliance forms reference
	Who chairs the SCCB?	
	______	
	Are SQA and SWCM members of the SCCB?	
	______	
5.8	13) There is a method for controlling trouble reports and tracking closures	
	______	
	There is a user's guide for the trouble report system	
	______	

Paragraph no.	Question	Objective evidence reference
5.12	14) Status on the SQA program is provided to the procuring agency	
	______	
	on a ______ basis	
	SQA milestones are structured to interweave with project/program milestones	
	______	
5.8	15) Do you currently use a PTR system?	
	______	
	SQA does check out the effectiveness of the software trouble report system used and tracks problems until they are closed	
	______	

Paragraph no.	Question	Objective evidence reference
5.9	16) SQA monitors the software development process against appropriate procedures that impact quality and the results are regularly provided to management. SQA assures that problems are closed-out	
	______	
	SQA is responsible for inspecting delivery packages to assure that they include:	
	proper media labels ____________________	
	labels contain part number ____________	
	labels contain content description ______	
	labels contain revision level ___________	
	labels contain contract no. ____________	
	Documentation necessary and sufficient to describe, install, and/or build the subject software product	
	______	

Additional comments:

Documents received:

Action items:

number	action	assignee

APPENDIX F:

SOURCE REFERENCE LISTINGS

Automated Tools

Tool	Source
CCC	SOFTOOL Corp. 340 South Kellogg Avenue Goleta, CA 93117 and 7799 Leesburg Pike Suite 900 Falls Church, VA 22043
Logiscope SQA Budget	AMS, Inc. 1525 Wilson Blvd. Arlington, VA 22209 (703) 841–7071
Master Planner	Strategic Financial Planning Systems, Inc. 6601 Little River Turnpike Suite 400 Alexandria, VA 22312 Attn: Clancy McQuigg
ASA	VERILOG 6303 Little River Turnpike Suite 340 Alexandria, VA 22312
Paperless PTR System	RDP, Inc. 391 Totten Pond Road Waltham, MA 02154 and 10640 Crestwood Drive Manassas, VA 22110

Other Points of Contact

IEEE Headquarters	345 47th Street New York, NY 10017–2394 (212) 705–7900 TELEX: 236411
IEEE Service Center	445 Hoes Lane Piscataway, NJ 08854–4150 (201) 981–0060 TELEX: 833233
IEEE Washington office	1111 19th St. N.W. Washington, DC 20036–3690 (202) 785–0017
ASQC	310 West Wisconsin Avenue Milwaukee, WI 53203 (414) 272–8575
ASQC Software Technical Committee	Point of Contact: Mr. Ed Ely Allen-Bradley Corp. (216) 449–6700

BIBLIOGRAPHY

Dobbins, J. H., and Buck, R. D. "Software Quality Assurance." *Concepts, The Journal of Defense Systems Acquisition Management* 5, No. 4 (Autumn 1982).

McCall, J.A. *The Utility of Software Quality Metrics in Large Scale Software System Developments*. Sunnyvale, Calif.: General Electric Company, 1978.

INDEX